A TRAILS BOOKS GUIDE

IOWA'S HOMETOWN FLAVORS

A FOOD LOVER'S TOUR

DONNA TABBERT LONG

TRAILS BOOKS
Black Earth, Wisconsin

Library of Congress Control Number: 2004115930
ISBN: 1-931599-54-8

Editor: Stan Stoga
Photos: Donna Tabbert Long
Design: Todd Garrett
Cover Photo: Paskus Studio

Printed in the United States of America by Versa Press, Inc.

10 09 08 07 06 05   6 5 4 3 2 1

Please Note: To avoid any disappointment, please call ahead before
setting out to the establishments listed in this book. Although we have
worked hard to ensure accuracy, establishments close and hours
of operation and other details change over time.

TRAILS BOOKS
A division of Trails Media Group, Inc.
P.O. Box 317 • Black Earth, WI 53515
(800) 236-8088 • e-mail: books@wistrails.com
www.trailsbooks.com

*To Angie, Rosemary, and Ruth—and everyone else who understands
what good road food is really all about.*

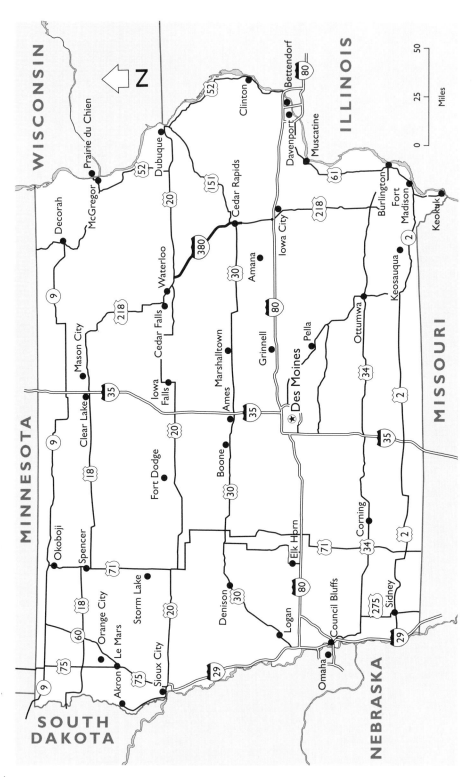

Contents

IV.   Des Moines:
Supper Clubs, Cinnamon Rolls, and the State Fair 73

V.   Northeast Region:
Pies, Picnics, and Norwegian Pancakes 99

VI.   East Central Region:
Kolaches and Dandelion Wine 119

VII. The Great River Road:

VIII. Southeast Region:

Introduction

Pork chops, pie, corn on the cob, Maytag blue cheese, loosemeat sandwiches, Amana wines, Dutch letters, and Muscatine melons—the bounty of Iowa is legendary. And then there is its world-renowned state fair, the granddaddy of all state fairs, where cinnamon roll competition is intense, and tasty pork tenderloins and corn dogs pervade.

Yet, like its landscape that varies from steep river bluffs to rolling fields of corn, Iowa offers up surprising platefuls of diversity too. Traversing the state, one discovers artisan breads being baked in Dubuque, fiery and spicy Thai dishes in Davenport, and aromatic Sri Lankan curries in Fort Madison. Indeed, Iowa today is loaded with tasty fare, and it's a rich blend of homegrown, homemade, and from the heart—no matter what language the heart speaks. Whether you're searching for the perfect piece of chocolate, an old-fashioned ice cream soda, or fresh sushi and kosher meats, Iowa boasts an abundance of worldly flavors and tastes just waiting to be dished up. The only prerequisite is that you may have to get off the interstate occasionally and follow the thin blue-squiggly lines on the map to get to them.

Iowa's Hometown Flavors: A Food Lover's Tour is designed to help you discover these sometimes off-the-beaten path culinary joys and pleasures. I hope the book entices you to search out the places where such offerings can be sampled: small town dining rooms, hip cafes, family-run steakhouses, generations-old orchards, pharmacies with soda fountains, and from-scratch bakeries. In addition to descriptions of food festivals, always an Iowa staple, I've also included tips about the best stores to stock up on picnic provisions, as well as sharing ideas for where to enjoy your alfresco feasts. A few favorite recipes from some of Iowa's most famous food companies and well-known chefs in the region are included too.

As a writer who loves reading about food almost as much as eating it, I hope that others will enjoy browsing this collection of Iowa's culinary gems—and cooks will discover a new recipe or two. But my main goal has been to produce a book that will serve as a useful tool for travelers looking to experience the real flavor that is Iowa.

Like my *Tastes of Minnesota* book, this is not a comprehensive state food guide by any means; it's personal and meant to be selective. My only regret is that due to time and word constraints, I could not include or even visit every place I wanted to. But the spots I do feature are the ones I truly love (with each and every one visited by me). None, by the way, has paid to be included in the book.

In selecting places to eat in each region, I also tried (where possible) to create a balance of eateries that represent a variety of dining styles, prices, and atmosphere: from a small bakery where you can pick up pastries for breakfast, to a lunch spot, to a dressier restaurant for dinner.

Over the past year, I've journeyed thousands of miles, crisscrossing the state. I've sampled warm apple pie late at night in my hotel room, eaten a few pork chops that tasted like shoe leather (yes, there were places that did not make the book), and sucked down three ice cream sodas in one afternoon. I also saw my first tractor parade, experienced my first cinnamon sticky rolls in a dinner breadbasket, and lost my glasses at a pumpkin farm (I found them). I only had to ride in a tow truck once after the car broke down.

Through it all, I've shared food, conversation, and laughter at too many tables to count and met many, many wonderful people. People who took the time to share their hopes, dreams, recipes, and stories with me. People whose culinary pride and craftsmanship is reflected in their lemon chiffon pies, their mashed potatoes, their grilled steaks, their blackberry sodas. These are folks who work long and hard and who need our support—so that road-tripping continues to be the delicious adventure it should be.

I had a great time. Now, it's your turn.

I wish you safe, fun-filled, and—as always—flavor-packed travels.

Acknowledgments

No book is the work of one person, and this one would never have happened without the advice, recommendations, help, and belief of many. Besides friends and family, I am indebted to countless people throughout Iowa who took the time to share their food knowledge and provide me with insights and nuggets of information that in many cases were unavailable in print.

Specifically, I want to thank Shawna Lode, of the Iowa Tourism Office, whose expertise and enthusiasm for Iowa shined apparent. She answered my questions, checked facts, provided information and contacts. Not only was she generous with her time and logistical support, but she did all of this with a smile, and I am deeply grateful to her. Thanks also go to the many other state tourism folks who helped me find my way around the state, providing guidance and sharing their time and tips.

Another thank you goes to my editor, Stan Stoga (whose patience knoweth no bounds). Others who need to be singled out: Mike Whye for helping by sending me tons of Iowa information, ideas, and suggestions; Lori Erickson for showing me her hometown, Iowa City; Stuart and Julie Oltrogge for showing me Clear Lake from the water, Liz Clark for inviting me into her home and sharing her recipes, and Wally and Paula Pasbrig for generously offering (without a minute's hesitation) the use of their car when mine broke down in the Amanas.

My "girlfriends forever" played a major role, serving as fellow travelers, timekeepers, and dining companions—sometimes eating lunch, pie, and chocolate shakes three times in a day—without complaints (usually!). Besides Angie Suchy, Ruth Martin, and Carole Peterson, I want to particularly thank Rosemary Holman for driving through wind and rain, bringing along coffee, coolers, towelettes, as well as pocket folders and carrying cases in her long-suffering quest to get me organized. I couldn't have done the book (and wouldn't have wanted to) without them along—for their laughter, navigational skills (or not), and constant moral support.

I want to offer special thanks to my mom, Edna Tabbert, for accompanying me too—and especially for being a good sport about that tow truck ride. Also, thanks to my sister, Sharon Melsheimer, who flew in from Nevada to share an Iowa fall weekend and put up with her little sister forgetting which hotel we had reservations at. For many reasons, I want to give a huge and heartfelt thank you to my family, but specifics that should be mentioned: my son David (and his buddy, Gus) for helping me out at the Iowa State Fair; my son Kevin for listening (and laughing in the appropriate places) to all my Iowa adventures on the phone, my son Keith and his wife, Rebecca, for showing me Decorah (and even sharing a B&B!). Last, but certainly never least, I am most grateful to my husband, Rod, whose support and love—and patience when deadlines loomed—carried me through once again to the finish line.

Northwest Region

Great Lakes, Ice Cream, and Popcorn

With its sparkling oases of lakes tucked into acres of waving cornfields, the northwest corner of Iowa is also a region where ice cream, candy, and barbecue sauce are produced. It's a land bountiful with summer memories, old boats, homemade root beer stands, and hot dog houses that have been grilling up the porky pink treats for decades.

Still, there's no doubt that the main attractions in northwest Iowa's Okoboji area are its glacier-carved lakes. Often referred to as the Iowa Great Lakes, they cover about 15,000 acres near the Minnesota border. Along with Iowa's largest natural lake, Spirit Lake, there are five others as well: West Okoboji, East Okoboji, Upper Gar, Lower Gar, and Minnewashta. But most everyone agrees, the spring-fed West Lake Okoboji is the centerpiece.

One of the reasons West Lake Okoboji has always been so beloved is the fact that Arnolds Park Amusement Park is located on its shores. Considered the oldest amusement park west of the Mississippi, Arnolds Park began its life in 1886 with a large slide that plunged into the lake. Today, the slide is gone, but there are plenty of other rides, including the 63-foot Ferris wheel that offers romantic views over the lake, and of course, the famous 1926 "Legend" wooden roller coaster—a definitive must for roller coaster aficionados.

Arnolds Park

In 1999, an expansive condo group made an offer to buy the then-struggling Arnolds Park Amusement Park. Thanks to strong community sentiment and support (they raised more than $7.6 million), Arnolds Park continues today as a retro step into the past. Added bonus: There's no entrance fee.

Whether you decide to visit the park or not, a stroll nearby the water here (especially lovely at sunset) is a summer tradition. Another must: You have to eat a famous Nutty Bar (a huge frozen block of vanilla ice cream, covered with chocolate and chopped peanuts, served on a stick). You can get one over at the Nutty Bar Stand (it's next door to Maxwell's Restaurant); the stand has been serving up this signature summertime Okoboji treat since 1945.

Likewise, the Black Walnut Candy Shop is another traditional stop. In business since 1919, they're now in their fifth generation of candy making—and kids today are still mesmerized watching through the window as the vintage taffy machine spins and pulls the sweet goo into soft and supple ropes that are later cut and hand-wrapped in waxed paper.

If you've been walking around the lakeshore long enough, you're also going to start wondering about the University of Okoboji (lots of "alums" here wearing emblazoned T-shirts). Here's the deal. Founded more than 20 years ago, the school was basically dreamt up (note the football team called the Phantoms) by three guys with an offbeat sense of humor. The joke took on a life of its own, and today there are U of O alumni chapters all over the country. If you want to be an "alum," head over to The Three Sons clothing store in Milford. A huge emporium, it has a complete section of U of O items—from pennants, shirts, and bumper stickers to baby outfits and water bottles.

Northwest Iowa is also home to the Ice Cream Capital of the World: Le Mars. This little slice of Mayberry features an ice cream museum, ice cream parlor, an almost 10-foot/tall ice cream sundae statue, and even garbage cans that look like ice cream cones. Le Mars's fame is due to the local Wells' Dairy—

A Nutty Bar is a summertime tradition in Okoboji country.

the world's largest family-owned dairy processor and producer of Blue Bunny Ice Cream. There's nothing finer than a stop here when the temp registers 94 degrees on the digital Blue Bunny temperature sign out front. (I should know.)

By the way, if you're in town toward the dinner hour, you also shouldn't miss Archie's Waeside. Since 1949, this well-regarded supper club has been a destination for steak lovers.

From Le Mars, it's a fast four-lane ride to the honey-producing Sioux City. Nudged up against Iowa's western border and located on the banks of the Missouri River, Sioux City offers its share of visually bothersome chain restaurants and fast food. But make your way downtown (do check out their Historic Fourth Street area) and take the time to search out a few of their signature eateries (Milwaukee Wiener House and Miles Inn come to mind), and you'll be assured fun and tasty experiences in this western Iowa town.

Sue Bee Honey History

In 1921, five beekeepers located near Sioux City, Iowa, formed a cooperative marketing organization with two hundred dollars and three thousand pounds of honey—and named it Sioux Honey Association (after the city of its founding).

In 1964, the Sioux Bee label on their honey was changed to Sue Bee to better reflect the correct pronunciation. Through the years, other lines of honey were added, including Clover Maid, Aunt Sue, Natural Pure, and North American brands. Today, Sioux Honey Association is a worldwide marketing organization.

Arnolds Park

Gepetto's
Central Emporium, Phone: (712) 332-2474

Talk about a meal with a view. Who would expect that at the back of this little mall (shops line the way there), Gepetto's opens up to a wall of windows with a spectacular view of West Lake Okoboji. Reserve a window table around sunset, and your rewards are many.

Even though the linens, the menu, the wine list, even the dressed-up servers, would all seem to imply this is a dress-up joint, the fact is many folks arrive here by boat. You can watch them tie up at the dock from your window-side table—the point being, except for maybe a dripping wet swimsuit, you can wear just about anything here. It's summer-wear casual.

But make no mistake, the menu is anything but summer casual. Read: no burgers in baskets, no beer in plastic cups. This is fine dining for folks who appreciate the good life—and good food.

Start out with an appetizer of the house—smoked chicken ravioli or Gepetto's mussels steamed in white wine. Either way, you'll want to sop up the lush sauces with some of the bread. Entrees here include everything from the standard Iowa prime rib (a huge hunk of meat) to roast duckling, lobster tail, grilled quail, and rack of lamb.

As for me, even with all the exotica, I love the simple pastas that Gepetto's does. A house-smoked salmon tossed with pasta and asparagus in a cream

Get a window seat at Gepetto's restaurant for a sunset view over West Lake Okoboji.

sauce is dauntingly rich, but totally delicious. Likewise, the item I think could be the best on the menu: veal saltimbocca. It's salty with prosciutto, and sultry sweet in veal stock and butter glaze.

Desserts are worth saving room for, too. But when the server brings out the tray with all the enticing choices, the decision is a tough one. My advice: If nothing else, share that creamy, caramel-y turtle cheesecake.

Tip: *Gepetto's is extremely busy every summer night. Make reservations— especially if you want a window table (although you can see the lake from just about anywhere in the room).*

O'Farrell Sisters
1302 Highway 71 N, Phone: (712) 332-7901

It takes a bit of hunting to find this well-worn white clapboard building— tucked a ways off Highway 71 in an established RV park.

So, I admit, I was a bit disappointed after the thrill of actually finding the place ("one block west of the bridge overlooking the bay"), to then discover that the O'Farrell sisters had sold their quirky establishment a few months before.

Not to worry. I'm happy to report that the current owner is keeping up the pie and pancake reputation that the sisters had worked hard to achieve. Best of all, the room hasn't been updated, either. Nostalgia for breakfast is a good thing.

The place has been an institution in the area since 1947, and the dining room feels like a 1950s vintage summer—with chrome and Formica tables and chairs, a counter that looks over those little travel-size boxes of cereal, and candy bar displays by the register.

The waitresses wear T-shirts displaying the "Original O'Farrell Sisters' Rules" (see sidebar), and keep your coffee cup (served on a saucer) filled every minute. The place is bustling on weekdays and packed on weekends. Plan to wait for a table.

But the wait is worth it. These pancakes are hot, fresh rounds—not doughy, but delicate, light, and satisfying as good pancakes should be. The rhubarb strawberry pie is also very fine, with its sweet-to-tart ratio the ultimate in country pie perfection. Nobody told me to have the cinnamon roll, but who could resist that Iowa-state-sized number on the counter? Thick with frosting, spicy with cinnamon, and warm from the oven, this is my idea of a marvelous morning repast.

The Original O'Farrell Sisters' Rules

- No eggs or oatmeal after 11
- No pie before 11
- No pie to go
- No scrambled or poached eggs
- Tables can't be moved . . . ever
- DPOTC (Don't Piss off The Cooks)

Smokin' Jakes
117 West Broadway, Phone: (712) 332-5152

Up the street from the amusement park (in Old Town) and a door down from Yesterdays, brick-fronted Smokin' Jakes is the best place in the Great Lakes region to find tender, tasty, Iowa-rich pork ribs. Slow roasted for hours over hickory logs, these meaty morsels (besides a rack of em', you can order them by the pail or the bucket) are so sweetly succulent, you may not even want to dip them in the rich, thick barbecue sauce that comes alongside.

By day, this casually rustic place has families filling its wood booths, ordering smokin' burgers topped with cheese and bacon, soups like the creamy baked potato, or fresh-from-the-garden greens piled high with plenty of smoked ham, turkey, pork, and/or chicken. 1919 Root Beer is on tap, along with Bud Light and Jake's Brew. Daylight diners can also check out the collection of antique bean pots (all stamped with the names of businesses that once gave them away as gifts to their customers) on the shelves that circle the room. Another collection of cast-iron cookware hangs on the wall over the bar.

Later in the afternoon, the vibe gets louder as the bar fills up. Then the "Evenin' Repasts" commence to be served. Platters of those baby back pork ribs, chops, or half a smoked chicken get dished up with sides of Jake's aromatic baked beans, coleslaw, or exemplary potato salad.

The happy hour crowd shows up around 10 p.m., when tap beers go for fifty cents until midnight. From midnight until 3 a.m.? You guessed it. Smokin' Jakes is the place for late-night breakfast after the party—and I've been told the biscuits and sausage gravy are stellar.

Spirit Lake

Goodies Handmade Candies
2321 30th Street, Phone: (800) 626-1078

When you see the sign for Goodies Handmade Candies on the east side of Highway 71 (in Center Lake Plaza), do make a point to turn in and stop. If you're here early in the day, you'll no doubt see the chocolates or the caramel being poured on the marble tables in back of the display counter. Intoxicating smells of butter and chocolate perfume the air.

This little operation began April 2, 1985. But business really began booming when the candy shop owner's baby son was born in June of that same year. The proud parents hung a banner out in front of the store proclaiming: IT'S A BOY! And amazingly, people started stopping in almost immediately, says David Tvedte.

Since then, like their son, the business has grown considerably. Today, the display case is filled with hand-dipped truffles. The dark Black Silk Truffle is their number-one seller (and for good reason), although I'm partial to the Buttery Truffle (all that pure creamery butter) and the Hazelnut variation: German hazelnut paste with milk chocolate, dusted in Dutch cocoa. Perhaps their most unusual truffle is the Lemon Meringue. David makes a lemon marmalade from scratch, bakes a meringue shell, then blends both into white chocolate, butter, and cream.

Don't miss the creamy caramels either, including the pinwheel version swirled with nougat—you hardly ever see these old-time candies anymore. Fudge is for sale here too; sample their Rilli Vanilli stuff even if you're not a big fudge fan.

Boxes of the creams, caramels, toffees, and fudge are available (you can order online as well) and range from a half pound to two pounds. My favorite is the University of Okoboji Alumni Assortment that also includes a University of Okoboji window sticker and one of the university's "entrance" exams.

Okoboji

Blue Moose Baking Company
East Oaks Mall, Phone: (712) 332-5727

Situated in the East Oaks Mall, this spacious shop is part art gallery—with some really cool paintings as offerings. It's a friendly sort of place where you'll find fresh-daily baguettes and baked goods. There's a decadent "round almond thing without a name" that you can order just like that—and they'll know what you mean. It's similar to a rich almond paste-filled coffeecake—an ultrasweet delight that actually goes quite well with a glass of merlot wine. And don't leave without a couple of their excellent scones (the chocolate chip or apricot studded are highlights). The Blue Moose is also a nice spot to relax and enjoy a healthy sandwich at lunchtime.

Spencer

Grantiques
307 Grand Avenue, Phone: (712) 262-6742

As you're heading through town, this little antique shop is right on the main drag. It is loaded with great old stuff, but what really sets this shop apart is that in the front of the store, next to the cash register, homemade cookies and cakes are for sale. There's even an old working Coke cooler that holds ice-cold bottles of orange soda and root beer. The owner of the shop bakes the sweet treats (try both the peanut butter and soft and spicy molasses cookies for sure) the old-fashioned way, "with real cream and butter," she says—to match the wares for sale in her store. As for the soda pop in bottles, they aren't the newfangled twist-off cap kind, so don't forget to open your bottle of pop the old-fashioned way as well: Use the Coca-Cola cooler's built-in bottle opener on its side.

Storm Lake

Abner Bell's Coffeehouse
210 East 5th Street, Phone: (712) 732-6142

When you're on the road and looking for a caffeine fix, this coffeehouse makes a great stop—especially if you're traveling through on a Friday, when you can get a coffee drink for free when you purchase a first-rate piece of, say, peach upside-down cake. But the coffeehouse offers lots more than just a cuppa and cake. There's Blue Bunny ice cream, there's pie, there are crunchy biscotti. There are sandwiches, there's soup. Need to check e-mail? All you have to do is ask, and they'll let you use their computer, gratis. There are newspapers to read, and comfy chairs to read them in. There are places to spread out a map and figure out where you're going. And there are friendly folks to ask if you don't know how to get there.

Ida Grove

Ida Grove Pharmacy
506 2nd Street, Phone: (712) 364-2734

This may be the only place in the state, heck, maybe in the world, where coffee still costs five cents. (Ten cents if you get it to go, according to the posted menu behind the soda fountain.)

But the reason most people stop in here is not for the coffee. It's for the beautiful and historic soda fountain that graces the front of the store—and serves up some serious ice cream treats. Banana splits, chocolate caramel malts, hot fudge sundaes, and lots more—including something called a Gedunk. According to Larry Albrecht, the former owner of this store (he still works in the pharmacy section several days a week), the Gedunk is a signature Ida Grove Soda Fountain delight. What exactly is it? It's a scoop of Blue Bunny vanilla ice cream, blanketed with chocolate syrup, followed by a scoop of chocolate ice cream heaped high with marshmallow cream—all served in the fluted, stemmed glass that ice cream sundaes should always be served in. With or without nuts, it's the best.

Ice cream treats and retro prices at the historic Ida Grove Soda Fountain and Pharmacy.

What's a Marshmallow Coke?

Pour some Coca-Cola almost to the top of a glass. Add a scoop of marshmallow cream. Stick a straw in, and the whole thing "explodes"—oozing and bubbling over the glass immediately. This was a favorite trick to play on new soda jerks (or those guys who thought they were so smart and knew it all), says Larry Albrecht, former owner of the Ida Grove Pharmacy. How did he learn about the concoction? "I had it done to me, of course," says Larry.

Now, about this soda fountain: Although the counter here no longer has the marble top (it broke years ago), underneath it's all marble—and the spectacular mirrored back bar, with "Olympia" in stained glass atop it, was brought down from the Olympia Candy Store in Sioux City in 1928. Complete with little green shaded lamps lighting the whole piece, this vintage soda fountain is the real thing. And its appeal hasn't changed one bit through the years.

Around 3 p.m., all the little kids come in, usually after the pool closes, said Jason Johnson (a nephew of the current owner) on the afternoon I visited. As he mixed up a strawberry Mountain Dew for one boy, another walked in. "Chocolate caramel?" asked Jason. The boy nodded. These were the regulars, I surmised, as more youngsters left their bikes outside and opened the door to enter.

Le Mars

Blue Bunny Ice Cream Parlor
20 5th Avenue SW (located at the Ice Cream Capital of the World Visitor Center), (712) 546-4522

From the 1920s reproduction ceiling tiles to the black-and-white vintage tiled floor, Blue Bunny's ice cream parlor is a step into yesterday. Half the fun is simply sitting at the 1904 antique Italian marble bar and reading the menu.

Sundaes include amazing concoctions like the Key Lime Melt Down: key lime ice cream layered with whipped vanilla mousse, key lime sauce, and graham cracker crumbs; or the Wildberry Safari: black raspberry ice cream with a blackberry revel and marionberry-filled chocolate mini cups. Kids go for the Kryptonice Cream: Super Hero Ice Cream covered in exploding Pop Rocks and smothered in whipped cream. And for real ice cream aficionados, of course, there's the Goliath: six scoops of your favorite flavor of ice cream, topped with whatever you choose: whipped cream, chocolate, hot caramel, marshmallow . . . don't forget the obligatory cherry on top.

Cool off at the Ice Cream Capital of the World in Le Mars.

Next door to the ice cream parlor, you can visit the ice cream museum (for a fee). It's popular with tour groups, so pay attention lest you get to the ice cream parlor just as the groups are finishing up their tour. (It conveniently exits almost directly into the soda fountain.) Kids also love the museum, especially the part where they can watch how ice cream drumsticks and Bomb-Pops are made dreaming and fantasizing and in some cases sharing aloud with complete strangers how and what they'd concoct if they could have an ice cream factory of their own.

A Bit of Blue Bunny History

Wells' Dairy was founded in 1913 by Fred H. Wells. Shortly thereafter, he and his brother, Harry C. Wells, formed a partnership and began to distribute ice cream in Sioux City, Iowa. In 1935, the brothers held a contest to find a name for their ice cream. A Sioux City man entered and won the $25 cash prize for his winning entry: Blue Bunny. (He got the idea after noticing his son enjoy the blue bunnies in a department store display window at Easter.)

Today, Wells' Dairy, Inc. is the largest family-owned and managed dairy processor in the United States, offering more than five hundred products and 50 flavors of ice cream. The most popular flavor? It's still vanilla. (But that's no surprise, because Blue Bunny offers five different flavors of vanilla!)

2004 Wells' Dairy, Inc. All rights reserved.

Bob's Drive-Inn
Highway 75 S, Phone: (712) 546-5445

Sure, you can get a Tavern here. You know, one of those loosemeat sandwiches that Iowa is famous for. But if you really know what you're doing at Bob's, you'll order one (or two) of their snap-to-the-bite hot dogs, spooned over with some of Bob's signature saucily-spiced loosemeat. Now you're cookin' with gas, as my mom would say.

Along with the hot dogs (extra bonus: at Bob's, the dogs and burgers are served on fresh bakery buns from the VanderMeer Bakery in town), you must order the onion rings—served with the obligatory ranch dressing out in these parts—and/or french fries. Both piles of these hot, crisp, fresh-fried treats are among the best I've tasted anywhere. I dream about this meal in the middle of winter. Get a thick and lovely malt or the house-made (from a secret family recipe) root beer here, and eat in the little room inside, or out back at a picnic table. Either way, someone is going to come by and ask how everything is, with genuine pride and care. This is a family-owned operation (Bob Kass opened the place in 1949 and it's still in the family) and it shows.

"I scream. You scream. We all scream. For pork tenderloin."
Seen on Burma Shave-type signs along a road in northwest Iowa.

Orange City

Woudstra Meat Market
117 Central Avenue NE, Phone: (712) 737-2913

This shiny-clean meat market in the Dutch community of Orange City is filled with pork chops and steaks, bologna and brats, and, of course, Dutch specialties like rings of fresh and smoked *metwurst*. Best of all, if you're wondering what to do with some of those Dutch offerings, you need only check the recipe box atop the meat market counter. Labeled "Kerry's Tried and True Recipe Box," there are free copies of cooking instructions inside for *metwurst*, as well as dozens of other recipes from Kerry Nieuwenhuis (meat market owner Norm Nieuwenhuis' wife). From grilled pork steak marinated in *Nederlanse* Marinade (available at Woudstra's) to Grandma's Meatballs made with Dutch rusks and flavored with a packet of *gehakt kruiden* (a Dutch meat spice), all the fixin's are available at Woudstra's.

If you're on the road and in the mood for a picnic, Woudstra's is also a nice place to pick up some of their well-spiced (and house-made) salami. Then, walk down to the Dutch Bakery (it's next to one of the few Ben Franklin stores left in the country), where you can select some bread or buns—and maybe a couple of those almond-rich Dutch Letters. The bakery also makes the brown, spicy Saint Nick cookies year round, but uses an antique windmill press for their shape. Pick up some bottles of Sioux City Sarsaparilla at the local grocery store, walk over to Windmill Park in the center of town, and indulge in a simple little outdoor feast.

Popcorn Ball Record

On June 12, 2004, forty-four volunteers and five staff members of Noble Popcorn Farms in Sac City "punched, packed, and carved" 910 pounds of popcorn with 1,500 pounds of sugar and 690 pounds of syrup, into a popcorn ball. The popcorn ball weighs 3,100 pounds, stands over 7 feet tall, and measures 23 feet in circumference.

This is not the first time these folks have attempted a record. In April 1995, they built a 2,225-pound popcorn ball to secure the title with Guinness. Later that same year, they were outdone by the local Boy Scouts. Although the Scouts' 1995 ball was blown up in 1997, the plans are to keep this record breaker, eventually housing it in its own building near the city's museum complex, creating a tourist attraction to enjoy right on Highway 20.

All this is no surprise. Noble Popcorn Farms is located in what has long been one of the finest popcorn-growing areas in the world.

Sioux City

Green Gables Restaurant
1800 Pierce Street, Phone: (712) 258-4246

A long-standing local classic, the Green Gables was also a favorite of the famous advice columnists Abigail Van Buren and the late Ann Landers. Sioux City natives, the two ate here when they were growing up and also made stops at the restaurant later when they were back in town visiting.

Now in its third generation of family ownership, this sprawling eatery—where you wait for a table on church pews—is part ladies' bridal luncheons, part deli, part diner, and part family gathering place. It features traditional, well-made Midwestern fare: hand-breaded pork tenderloins are immense, the chicken salad legendary. They also serve from-scratch matzoh ball soup and show-stopping ice cream extravaganzas—like their H-Bomb. A bizarre sort of concoction, it's part soda (choose raspberry), part sundae. It's messy and gushy, loaded with ice cream and heaped high with piles of whipped cream. Two straws—each adorned with half a cherry—stick out of the soda glass. It's definitely a dessert you need to share.

Palmer's Olde Tyme Candy Shoppe
209 Douglas Street, Phone: (712) 258-7790

The factory that once churned out tantalizing treasures is no longer located here, but you can still make out the fading print on the side of the tall brick building where Palmer's Olde Tyme Candy Shoppe is now located: "Palmer Candy Co. Makers of Pure Candy. Palmer's Chocolates. Quality Unexcelled."

Open the heavy old door to the candy shop here, and Willy Wonka fans will be overcome with giddiness. Tables and tables filled with boxes and boxes of chocolates to be scooped and bagged up, bulk style: chocolate-covered raisins, chocolate-covered peanuts, vanilla creams . . . There are bags of gummi delights, jelly beans, and shelves filled with jars loaded with a colorful assortment of every old-fashioned kind of candy you can think of: licorice snaps, butterscotch, lollipops, and more. Besides displays of Valomilk bars, there are boxes of Twin Bing candy bars in bulk—and sweatshirts and hats with Palmer Candy logos too. Interestingly enough, for some reason, the light that falls through the glass blocks into the room here seems

In 1923, the Palmer Candy Company's Bing candy bar was born in Sioux City; 50 years later, the Twin Bing was introduced.

to shed a flattering magical quality over the whole scene—including the tiny-tiled floor. It almost does feel a little like you're in a movie.

While the kids are out of their minds trying to choose, parents can enjoy perusing the Palmer Candy history in huge framed photos that are on the walls—along with actual displays of some of the old candy-making equipment. But don't think mom and dad are leaving without their favorite stash of sweets, too.

The Bing's Beginnings

Begun in 1878, The Palmer Candy Company started out with the Palmers selling bulk and hard candy in wooden containers from the back of their Sioux City fruit house. By 1900 they had outgrown these humble beginnings and moved into the four-story building in downtown Sioux City—the current site of the candy shop. At that time, the owners were very proud of their quite modern facility, which boasted such up-to-date technology as ammonia cold storage and its own electric generator and steam boilers.

In 1923, when candy bars were cutting-edge novelties, the birth of Palmer Candy's Bing candy bar took place. The Bing was launched initially with four flavors: pineapple, maple, cherry, and vanilla. Today, the cherry Bing candy bar is still produced, along with the double bump Twin Bing, which was introduced in 1973, and the triple-bump King Bing in 1986.

Considered one of the country's oldest candy companies, Palmer's also has the longest span of family ownership and management of any candy company of its size in the United States. The great great grandson of founder E. C. Palmer runs the Palmer Candy Company today. The business has no plans to slow down either—in 2003 a new 220,000-square-foot-facility was purchased to be renovated into a state-of-the-art plant.

Pierce Street Coffee Works
1920 Pierce Street, Phone: (712) 255-1226

Deep reds, bright yellows, retro chintz tablecloths, and stars hanging from a purple painted ceiling all work together at this bustling neighborhood coffeehouse. In the morning there are plates of scones and muffins, or you can get a nice little dish of fresh yogurt scattered with Grape Nuts. Besides the regular lattes and espressos, Pierce Street offers combos like the Funky Squirrel (honey and hazelnut latte) or As Good as Disco (créme de cocoa and vanilla mocha). Local artwork on the walls changes often.

Even if you're not a caffeine junkie, put this shop on your list for a lunchtime sandwich stop. Choose from topnotch breads, several meats, a couple cheeses, a few vegetables, and lots of extras like cranberry sauce or hot peppers. The caring and friendly staff does a nice job here.

Sarah's Candies
518 Pierce Street, Phone: (712) 277-0550

Tucked next door to Sioux City's recently renovated Orpheum Theatre, this candy shop is like a sweet little secret. If you're here in the morning you may even catch owner Sarah Herwynen whipping up some of her ultra rich peanut butter cups or buttery English toffee in the tiny kitchen behind the cash register.

The display counter is filled with enticing confections: cashew and pecan caramels; almond and peanut clusters; vanilla caramels; cherry, maple, and raspberry creams; chocolate-covered orange peels; and peanut brittle. Name-brand candies, including Jelly Belly jelly beans are also for sale, and decorative tins for gift giving.

Herwynen also carries Annaclairs, although she doesn't make them. They have a soft, sweet center with pecans and chocolate around it, says Herwynen—and they used to be one of the chocolates that the Younkers department store carried when they still had a candy kitchen. She decided to sell them at her shop when so many people kept asking about them.

In addition, the store buys the finest nuts—almonds, cashews, and the like—and roasts them daily. Besides the standard peanuts and pistachios in the shell, you can buy pepitas here. These are Mexican pumpkin seeds, and they're an addictive little treat. Herwynen also makes several varieties of nutty mixes, including a South of the Border blend (slightly spicy), a Cheddar Parmesan Delight, and a popular Hawkeye Mix—a mildly sweet and salty blend of pepitas, peanuts, and cashews.

Sioux City's Historic Fourth Street

Just east of the railroad yards at the intersection of 4th and Court Streets in Sioux City is the newly renovated, two-block section referred to as Historic Fourth Street. Once an old warehouse district, today the beautiful buildings built between 1889 and 1915 (many in the Richardson Romanesque style) have been restored and house boutique shops, brewpubs, live music clubs, and several worthy restaurants. Along with the Victorian Opera House, there's Buffalo Alice (recommended for pizza and their spaghetti sauce), there's Sweet Fanny's (walls covered with World War II memorabilia and serving good French onion soup), Tom Fooleries for great burgers, and Luciano's for Italian specialties.

Miles Inn
2622 Leech Avenue, Phone: (712) 276-9825

This corner 1925 brick building is a typical neighborhood tavern all right, but the place doesn't sell the ubiquitous Iowa sandwich under that name. Here the Tavern or loosemeat sandwich goes by the name Charlie Boy. (Named after Charlie Miles, who was founder John Miles's son.)

These hot and spicy—I once heard someone refer to them as "pepperly" (an apt description)—numbers are served with mustard and pickles. Be fore-warned: They are absolutely addictive.

So do yourself a favor and order a couple upfront at the bar—to go if you don't want to sit inside with the noise and commotion. But if you want the whole experience, you really must sit at the bar, eat at least two of these flavorful sandwiches, and wash it all down with an ice-cold schooner (or two) of beer.

Largest Ice Cream Sandwich

According to the Guinness Book of World Records, Hy-Vee, Inc., in conjunction with Wells' Blue Bunny, Metz Baking Company, and Giese Sheet Metal, made an ice cream sandwich weighing 1,115.8 kilograms (2,460 pounds) in Dubuque, Iowa, on February 27, 1998.

Milwaukee Wiener House
309 Pearl Street, Phone: (712) 277-3449

Known to generations (it's been around for more than 80 years) for its hot dogs, the Milwaukee Wiener House is an institution around Sioux City. Kids grow up and bring their kids back here for a simple Saturday lunch of grilled and hot, hot dogs on cushy warm buns, cold Coke in a bottle stuck with a straw, and maybe a mini bag of good ol' potato chips.

The place appears small from the outside, but looks deceive. Inside, the room, with its slippery plastic booths lining the walls, seems to go back a mile. And it's usually jam-packed.

But the first thing you see when you walk in here is not the spacious digs, but the grill loaded with all those little pinkish doggies nestled together in perfect formation. There's no time to think: Get yourself in the line (there's always a line) and order your hot dog. With "everything" gets your dog spooned over with that juicy loosemeat mixture, a squirt of mustard, and a load of chopped onions—all efficiently and expertly put together by one of the several guys

Known to generations (it's been around for more than 80 years), the Milwaukee Wiener House is an institution in Sioux City.

behind the counter, wearing their white aprons and those cute little paper hats. If you want, you can get a BowWow (two dogs in one bun) or a Barker (hot dog with sauerkraut). Next, order your bottle of soda pop. Get the bag of chips; add it to your tray. Pay your bill and go sit down. It's cheap. It's fast. It's fun. And it's really delicious.

Tastee Inn and Out Drive-In
2610 Gordon Drive, Phone: (712) 255-0857

Famous for their onion chips served with creamy ranch dressing, this old drive-in with its big neon sign out front is another Sioux City institution.

Jolly Time Pop Corn

JOLLY TIME Pop Corn began in the Sioux City basement of Cloid H. Smith in the year 1914. At that time a grocer wishing to sell popcorn had to buy it in bulk or purchase it still on the cob and there was no guarantee the kernels would even pop!

Smith decided to produce and package high-quality popcorn that would be consistent from one bag to the next to sell to grocery stores. The family picked the popcorn from their farm, moved it by wagon to Sioux City, and then shelled, cleaned, and graded it in their home. The first year they sold over 75,000 pounds of popcorn and made JOLLY TIME Pop Corn the first brand name in popcorn!

Now in the fourth generation of the Smith family, the company continues to be successful—and its products can be found across the United States and in 24 foreign countries.

Smith Family's Famous Baked Caramel Corn

2 bags popped JOLLY TIME Microwave Pop Corn
   (about 21 to 24 cups)
Nonstick cooking spray
1 cup (2 sticks) butter or margarine
2 cups firmly packed brown sugar
$1/2$ cup light or dark corn syrup
1 teaspoon salt
$1/2$ teaspoon baking soda
1 teaspoon vanilla

Preheat oven to 250 degrees. Coat the bottom and sides of a large roasting pan with nonstick cooking spray. Place popped popcorn in roasting pan (removing any unpopped kernels). In a heavy pan, slowly melt butter; stir in brown sugar, corn syrup, and salt. Heat to a boil, stirring constantly; boil without stirring for 5 minutes. Remove from heat; stir in baking soda and vanilla. Gradually pour over popped popcorn, mixing well. Bake for 1 hour, stirring every 15 minutes. Remove from oven, cool completely. Break apart and store in a tightly covered container.

Makes about 24 cups.

Optional: Mix in one 8-ounce package of whole almonds or pecan halves before baking.

Easy Microwave Caramel Corn

1 bag popped JOLLY TIME Microwave Pop Corn
  (about 10-12 cups)
$1/3$ cup butter or margarine
$2/3$ cup firmly packed brown sugar
$1/3$ cup light corn syrup
$1/4$ teaspoon baking soda
$1/2$ teaspoon vanilla

   In 4-quart microwave-safe glass bowl, microwave butter on high until melted, about 45 seconds. Stir in brown sugar and corn syrup. Microwave on high until mixture boils, 1 to 3 minutes, stirring once. Microwave on high 2 to 3 minutes without stirring. Stir in soda and vanilla. Stir in popped popcorn (removing any unpopped kernels), mixing well. Microwave on high 1 minute. Remove and stir. Microwave on 70 percent power for an additional minute. Remove from oven; stir again to coat popcorn evenly. Cool completely on cookie sheet. Break apart.
   Makes about 10 cups.
   Recipes courtesy of JOLLY TIME Pop Corn and reprintedwith permission.

Along with their loosemeat sandwiches (they call theirs Tastees here) and root beer, this drive-in was Sioux City's original fast food-serving to families on Friday nights long before the golden arches arrived. Ask any local and they'll probably have memories of the drive thru "shopper's special": 12 Tastee loosemeat sandwiches, a huge bucket of fries, and a half gallon of root beer. Enough food to feed the fam and a few neighborhood kids to boot—for under $20.

   Today, the shopper's special is still on the menu, still under $20, and still a mighty fine Friday night treat.

Wall Lake

Cookies Food Products, Inc.
3444 Mace Avenue, Phone: (712) 664-2662

Wall Lake may be the birthplace of Andy Williams, but I suspect these days more people associate it with the award-winning Cookies Barbeque Sauce.
   Founded in 1975 by L.D. Cook (his nickname was "Cookie"), the business

began in the corner of the Wall Lake Fire Department garage. After three months, the company moved to the west edge of Wall Lake—where it is still located, although it has expanded in size.

Iowa, where fields of opportunity await.

Today, Cookies Food Products are distributed in 32 states and even exported to Mexico. Besides its original smoky sweet sauce, it also manufactures Cookies Western Style version (less sweet, but minced onion and cayenne pepper give it a zip), plus two kinds of taco sauce, several seasoning blends, and even a couple salsas. Cookies Western Style sauce won the title of Best Sauce on the Planet at the American Royal Barbecue, the world's largest barbeque sauce contest, held annually in Kansas City. Thirty-five-thousand people, including 327 barbeque teams, attended the two-day event—the largest competition in the country, making it the largest barbeque contest in the world!

You can visit and tour the barbeque plant in Wall Lake and pick up plenty of Cookies products in the store there. Their Web site features all kinds of recipes using their products as well. See the sidebar for one of the best.

Cookies Double Smoked Ham

6-to 8-pound bone-in ham with natural juices (may be spiral sliced)

1 cup Cookies Western Style BBQ Sauce

1 cup Cookies Original Style BBQ Sauce

1/4 cup pure maple syrup

3 tablespoons Rose's Lime Juice (may substitute real lemon or
   lime juice)

Set ham cut-side down in 9x13-inch pan. Start your gas grill and heat up to 200 to 250 degrees. Make packet of hickory chips in foil. (About the size of your fist.) Poke several holes in the foil with a fork. Lay packet on lava rocks or flavorizer bars. Set pan with ham in on top of grates. Smoke for 3 to 4 hours. Make sure grill gets no hotter than 250 degrees. Drain off liquid and reserve for delicious ham gravy. Mix together the sauces, syrup, and Rose's Lime Juice. Pour over ham in the pan and return to the grill. Have grill no hotter than 200 degrees. Leave on grill for approximately 45 minutes while you are making the ham gravy. Remove from grill. Slice and serve. Best ham you will ever eat!

Ham Gravy

Pan juices from roasting the ham

flour

water or milk

Pour off the juices into a 4 to 6 cup measuring cup that will stand hot liquid. Skim off $1/2$ cup of the clear, oily liquid (the fat). Pour the $1/2$ cup fat into a saucepan or deep frying pan. Mix with $1/2$ cup all-purpose flour. Cook over medium heat until it bubbles. Skim off the remaining fat from the pan juices. Add to those juices enough water or milk to make 4 cups. Gradually add that to the flour and fat in the saucepan, stirring constantly until it boils and thickens. Makes approximately 12 servings.

Optional: Add 1 tablespoon Cookies Flavor Enhancer to the gravy.
Recipe courtesy of Cookies Food Products and reprinted with permission.

Chuck Offenburger's Delightful Dozen Iowa Food Favorites

For 21 years, Chuck Offenburger wrote the "Iowa Boy" column four times per week for the *Des Moines Register*, before leaving to teach and do freelance writing. Today, he writes for the Web site www.Offenburger.com.

I can't possibly just pick 10 places in Iowa that are my favorite places to eat.

Regina's, Fairfield. The favorite of the local transcendental meditators and non-meditators alike, maybe the finest restaurant in Iowa, with my favorite entree being the salmon on a flaming wood shingle.

Breitbach's Country Dining, Balltown. Iowa's oldest restaurant and bar dating to the late 1850s, for their buffet and, especially, their red raspberry pie.

Stone's Restaurant, Marshalltown. Iowa's second oldest restaurant, dating to 1887, for their general menu but especially their Mile High Lemon Chiffon Pie.

Winga's Café, Washington. Operated by the Winga family in southeast Iowa for 75 years, famous for their cornmeal mush.

The Sanctuary, Shenandoah. Mary Peterson's lemon coconut pie.

Abner Bell's Coffeehouse, Storm Lake. Karen Grieme's " chicken wrap" sandwiches.

China Cafe, Johnston. It's all good, but my favorite is probably the cashew chicken.

Northwestern Steakhouse, Mason City. Best steaks in the state.

Green Gables, Sioux City. For 75 years the favorite of Sioux Citians and visitors who learn about it, especially for their two unusual menu items of matzoh ball soup and liver and onions.

Pepper Sprout, Dubuque. A relatively new place that is tremendous with its "Fine Midwest Cuisine" menu.

Taylor's Maid-Rite, Marshalltown. Famous for their Maid-Rite sandwiches and malts. Their Maid-Rites, incidentally, are made from beef that is cut from the carcasses, which hang in the basement cooler, and ground on the spot.

Peony Chinese Restaurant, Jefferson. The Mandarin beef is tops.

Southwest Region
Town Squares and Soda Fountains

Along with the rolling Loess (rhymes with bus) Hills in southwest Iowa, this corner of the state is dotted with pretty town squares—complete with courthouses and clock towers. Folks frequent hometown cafés, crowd into bakeshops for bread, and sit at old-fashioned soda fountains for strawberry shakes.

In fact, the region boasts more than its fair share of old-fashioned soda fountains—the *real* kind—found in pharmacies. Besides McMahon Drug in tiny Corning, there's the George Jay Drug in Shenandoah, Tyler Pharmacy in Lenox, and Penn Drug in Sidney—the oldest family-run drugstore in Iowa. These are all cool places (literally and figuratively) to share a hot fudge sundae, a refreshing Green River phosphate, or a chocolate malt. But remember: If you ask for a soda in these parts, you'll end up with the ice cream kind. If you're looking for a Coke, ask for the varieties of "pop" the place carries. And if you're really a Coca-Cola lover, make sure you hit Atlantic (the "Coca-Cola Capital of Iowa") on the fourth weekend of September when their Coca-Cola Days takes place.

Iowa's Speed Limit

"The laws of Iowa hold that a motor vehicle must be so driven in a careful and prudent manner so as not to endanger the property of another or life and limb of any person. A speed in excess of 25 miles an hour is presumptive evidence that an automobile is not being so driven."
-from "The Complete Official Road Guide of The Lincoln Highway, 1916"

Bronco bustin' (check out the rodeos in Sidney and Lenox) is popular in this region of horse ranches too, but the area is home to several more refined celebrations as well. Every June, the friendly and pretty small town of Clarinda celebrates the life of their hometown hero—and the Big Band era's most popular leader—Glenn Miller. Arrive a day before the festival, take a wander past Miller's birthplace home, and you might even hear piano notes as somebody tunes up Miller's piano. The annual event includes bands from around the world, along with picnics featuring homemade ice cream, and the proverbial pancake breakfast. (And don't leave town without a stop at the Bakery on the square for possibly the best cinnamon rolls in the county.)

More musical roots can be found in Shenandoah, the boyhood stomping

The Loess Hills Scenic Byway winds its way through the unique Loess Hills in western Iowa.

grounds of the famous Everly Brothers. If you're a fan, you'll want to stop in at the old train station that's been converted into a restaurant. The place is loaded with the singers' memorabilia, and you can sit out on the loading platform to eat (don't be surprised to hear your server's mom went to school with the Everly boys). Be aware that occasionally a real train does roar by. Food here is decent and down-home good.

In south central Iowa, the actress Donna Reed (America's favorite mom—the one who was always dressed to her pearl earrings for breakfast) grew up on a farm near Denison. She returned often, even after she was a star. In honor of its famous offspring, each June Denison hosts the Donna Reed Performing Arts Festival. This is when workshops feature nationally known directors, writers, and producers.

No matter when you're here, however, take time to peek inside the gorgeously restored German Opera House (where performances and movies take place). Then make a stop at Reiney's Soda Fountain and Candy Kitchen next door. Order a hot fudge sundae, and don't forget to check out the window where, years ago, "Irene

Hideaway Picnic Spots

Hideaway picnic spots abound in this deep corner of the state, but you've got to get off the beaten path to find them. Near Thurman, there is Waubonsie State Park with its scenic overviews and hiking trails along the Loess Hills. (There's also a hunting lodge where they serve meals on weekends.) Just west of Glenwood, there is Pony Creek Park and West Oak Forest. These are remote places, simple areas where you can walk a trail or savor a cup of hot apple cider from a thermos amidst the bliss of country quiet.

In the autumn, head north on Highway 183 from CB toward Crescent (check out the Pink Poodle supper club if you're a steak lover) and on to Missouri Valley, or "Mo Valley," as the locals call it. You'll pass by country streets with endearing names like Honeysuckle Road, Holly Lane, and Honey Creek. It's a lovely, tree-shaded drive (near the old Lincoln Highway) that curves gently through countryscapes that calm the soul and refresh the heart.

Onawa: Birthplace of the Eskimo Pie

The first ice cream bar was created by Christian Kent Nelson in Onawa, Iowa. In 1920, he watched as a young customer was having difficulty choosing between an ice cream sandwich and a chocolate bar. Nelson decided to create a solution—the chocolate covered ice cream bar on a stick. He originally called it the I-Scream-Bar. It was popular immediately, and in 1921 Nelson partnered with Russell C. Stover (the candy maker) to produce the treat, which they renamed the Eskimo Pie.

Topping" scratched her name in the glass with a diamond ring.

Huge, glitzy casinos abound around Council Bluffs, but take a drive downtown and you'll find friendly cafés like Duncan's, where they've been serving up hospitality and homespun fare for years. Craving a double skim latte (extra foam)? Head nearby to the Steam N Koffee—a coffeehouse by day and musical venue by night. For simple but good lunches, head to Barley's, or Scott Street Pub. Tish's is another recommended noon-time spot. If the weather is nice, pick up lunch at the Taste of China, where the food is made to order, stir-fried in front of you, then head over to nearby Bayliss Park for a picnic lunch.

South of CB, bicyclists love to explore the Wabash Trace Nature Trail, a great 63-mile trail stretching between CB and the small town of Blanchard on the Iowa-Missouri border. Following an old railroad bed through the Loess Hills, the trail's gentle inclines make for perfect walking and biking—with plenty of small towns to stop in and sip a cool one or grab something good to eat. In fact, the tiny town of Mineola is about 10 miles south of Council Bluffs—and its Mineola Steakhouse has become something of a cult destination with bicyclists, especially on Thursdays when they have cheap tacos.

Denison

Reiney's Soda Fountain
1301 Broadway, Phone: (712) 263-4752

Oh, what ice cream delights to savor in this renovated soda fountain! My favorite is the Turtle Sundae (Blue Bunny vanilla ice cream drizzled over with creamy caramel, thick hot fudge, chopped pecans—topped off with a whirl of whipped cream and a cherry with a stem.) Then again, I also like the Roof Tin—scoops

Reiney's Soda Fountain is housed in the same building as the Donna Reed Center.

of chocolate ice cream oozing marshmallows, crunchy with nuts. I can't think of anything cooler on a sultry summer afternoon than spooning up such cold comfort, except maybe sipping a refreshing Pink Lady phosphate in between bites.

Housed in the Donna Reed Center for the Performing Arts (on the historic corner of Broadway and Main), Reiney's original candy kitchen was renovated and reopened in 1995 as this old-time soda fountain. With its pink marble counter top dating from 1907 (it was purchased from a Chicago deli), Reiney's history is a rich one.

"When this was the candy shop, I can remember my mom coming in here at Christmastime and buying bags of their homemade anise candy," says Renee Short, scooping out ice cream behind the counter on one of the days I visited. "At lunchtime, they also had these little tiny hamburgers they made that were the best." And yes, this was the place for "date night" when she was a teenager.

Today, points out Short, the renovated shop still has the dumbwaiter once used to bring up the chocolates and ice cream made in the basement. The dumbwaiter also hauled up the workers at that time; the flight of stairs in the corner now was added when the store reopened in the mid-1990s.

After you've indulged yourself with ice cream, take time to stroll through the adjacent Center. A miniature replica of Bedford Falls, the town from the movie *It's a Wonderful Life*, is on permanent display. And if it's open, do sneak more than a peek in the ornate theater.

Diamonds and Ice Cream

"Back in the 1930s an employee of Jim and Mami Bartholomew in the candy kitchen received a diamond ring from her boyfriend. Checking to see if it was real, she etched her name in the glass of one of the doors of the show window at the front of the store. The name 'Irene Topping' and the window has survived all these years!" Check it out.
-*sign on the front window of Reiney's Soda Fountain in Denison*

Bedford

Junction Café
804 Pollock Boulevard, (712) 523-2454

Adjacent to a Beemer Oil station, the only indication that this café might be anything extraordinary is the sign out front boasting it as the "home of legendary strawberry shortcake." Indeed, the strawberry shortcake is wonderful here, but there are plenty more things to recommend the place—including the huge cinnamon rolls in the morning, the hand-patted juicy burgers at lunch, the homemade biscuits and sausage gravy at suppertime, and the fantastic repertoire of tasty pies (lemon meringue, gooseberry, strawberry rhubarb, coconut cream) anytime in between. Oh, and did I mention the High Plains Bread Pudding Warm With Sauce? It's sublime, sturdy, sweet, Midwest fare.

Coffee is still fifty cents at the Junction, and mid-morning, locals in seed caps and overalls fill the booths. This is the type of place where near the cash register (on the horseshoe-shaped counter), you'll see locally authored books and plastic bags full of homemade chocolate nut clusters for sale. On occasion, a glance under the counter could net you a pair of worn but still perfectly wearable

Is there any doubt what the signature dish is at the Junction Café in Bedford?

cream-colored cowboy boots, with a hand-lettered sign stating, "Size 10^1/$_2$ D for sale, $15."

Friday nights there's the weekly fish supper: Alaskan pollock or Gulf shrimp complete with potato, salad, and biscuit for under five bucks. And Saturday nights there's always musical entertainment.

The café and adjacent dining room are filled with ranch décor: ropes and spurs, plus photos of the café owners Everette and Betty Lee's prize-winning colts. Shelves of trophies are from their horse showings as well. (The Lees also own the horse ranch, Rockin' Diamond—which is only a half mile from their café. The proximity of the two keeps them busy—sometimes working with a newborn foal in the morning, then cleaning up and helping with the noon meal at the café.) Betty is the one responsible for those pies, by the way, as well as the ham balls (popular at Sunday dinners).

Strawberry Shortcake Brings 'em In

When the Lees purchased the Junction Café in 1992, they made some changes. Some worked. Some didn't. Their large strawberry shortcake was one that definitely worked. For three years they gave one away daily on a local radio station—which proved to be a great way to advertise and promote the product as well as the restaurant. The first day the Lees sold the shortcake was Memorial Day 1993— selling 72 on that day alone.

Elk Horn

Jacquelyn's Danish Bake Shoppe and Kaffe Hus
4234 Main Street, Phone: (712) 764-3100

On Saturdays, a stop in this cheerful spot for an *aebleskiver* breakfast is worth the detour. (It's also the only day they're served.) What exactly are aebleskivers?

Danish Windmill

Elk Horn's 60-foot windmill, built in Denmark in 1848, was dismantled and shipped to Elk Horn, where it was rebuilt in 1976 by community volunteers to honor the area's Danish heritage. Visitors can climb to the top of the mill, see the grinding stones, and watch the wings go around on a windy day. Later, don't forget to purchase some wheat or rye stone-ground flour.

Elk Horn's famous Danish windmill.

They're the Danish version of pancakes—and they look a little like baseballs. If you've never tasted one, this is the place to start.

Even if you're here on a weekday you can't go wrong with a "kaffe" break at Jacquelyn's. Select a flaky lemon pinwheel or an airy pillow of a Danish almond puff, a cup of strong, well-made coffee, then have a seat inside or at a sidewalk table out front.

Jacquelyn also makes Danish breads (pumpernickel, dark, and light rye), Danish Letters, and the buttery, melt-on-the-tongue pastry known as kringle.

Elk Horn Foodtown
4141 Main Street, Phone: (712) 764-8251

Home of At-A-Boy Roy's Specialty Meats, this little old grocery store is unlike any other. What small convenience store do you know that stocks *rullepolse*, pressed chicken, dried beef, Danish rye bread, and makes its own *medisterpolse*, liver pate, summer sausage, and bacon? Don't leave without at least some of Roy's Beef Jerky. It's chewy, tasty and addictive.

Danish Inn
4116 Main Street, Phone: (712) 764-4251

For those who miss Elk Horn's Tivoli Fest (held Memorial Weekend, it's a celebration of the town's Danish heritage), not to worry. You can still sample

A Food-Friendly Place to Stay

Joy's Morning Glory Bed and Breakfast
4308 Main Street
Phone: (712) 764-5631; (888) 764-5631

Bright flowers line the walkway to Joy and Merle Petersen's 1912-era home in Elk Horn, where the welcome is heartfelt and warm. Antiques abound within, and Joy's collections all have a story—from the restored cookstoves and nostalgic kitchenware to the family china in the heirloom cabinet.

Still, the best part about staying here is that in the morning you awaken to the scent of breakfast quiche and cinnamon-spiked muffins wafting up the stairs and into your room. Downstairs, the dining room table is set with vintage patterned plates and glassware that sparkles in the morning sunshine. Along with quiche, fresh fruit is served in an antique sherbet dish. The coffee is strong and good, and the muffins are warm from the oven.

Joy's Morning Glory Muffins

1 1/4 cups sugar

2 1/4 cups flour

1 tablespoon cinnamon

2 teaspoons baking soda

1/2 tablespoon salt

1/2 cup shredded coconut

1/2 cup raisins

1 apple, shredded

3 ounces crushed pineapple, drained

2 cups grated carrots

1/2 cup pecans

Whisk in separate bowl:

3 eggs

1/2 cup oil

1/2 cup applesauce

1 teaspoon vanilla

Mix all together. Blend well. Fill muffin tins 3/4 full, and bake at 350 degrees for 35 minutes. These freeze well too.
Recipe courtesy of Joy Petersen and reprinted with permission.

a smorgasbord of Danish food specialties here at the Danish Inn year-round. Try frikadeller (meatballs), medisterpolse (sausage), rod kaal (red cabbage), agurkesalat (sliced cucumber salad) and ris a l'amande (rice pudding); they're always on the menu. So are a variety of traditional Danish open-faced sandwiches served on home-baked Danish rye bread. Unsure what to order? You can't beat the buffet—besides pork roast stuffed with prunes and apples, red cabbage, and Danish meatballs, there's also mashed potatoes and broasted chicken.

Woodbine

Eby Drug Store
423 Walker Street, Phone: (712) 647-2840

The soda fountain in this 1916 drugstore is not as charming (no marble counter; plus they use paper products for serving their phosphates and floats), but it's still fun to visit, if only because Woodbine is such a pretty little town. (Woodbine has re-laid all of its downtown sidewalks with brick to match the oldest remaining brick segment of the Lincoln Highway; see sidebar.)

Here you can get a key lime pie malt, then take it along while you wander through the White Floral Gardens at Eleventh and Park Streets in town. This is a well-maintained, tree-shaded park filled with peonies and greenery.

Woodbine's Historic Highway

Lincoln Way is significant as part of the original transcontinental U.S. Highway 30, and it was bricked in the summer of 1921. Today in Woodbine, Lincoln Way's 11 blocks are the largest remaining original portion of Lincoln U.S. Highway 30 in Iowa. It's on the National Register of Historical Places and is used as a main thoroughfare for traffic through Woodbine.

Corning

McMahon Drug
625 Davis Avenue, Phone: (641) 322-3454

There's nothing like stepping inside this cool oasis of ice cream delight—especially when the heat/humidity index is in the Iowa "tropical" zone. Beyond the spin-around displays of sunglasses and paperback books, and next to the wall-length windows looking out on downtown Corning's main drag, is the soda fountain. Behind it and above the mirror is a huge bright red sign advertising Coca-Cola.

But Coca-Cola is beside the point at this place. What you want to order here is a jewel-toned black raspberry soda served in a vintage fluted soda glass—with a long-handled spoon and a straw. Or maybe a Majestic Milky Way Milk Shake made with Iowa's Blue Bunny ice cream. Then you just want to dawdle over it—making it last as long as you can.

Opened in 1910, this is the kind of drugstore where town kids have been congregating for years—drinking phosphates that range from the classic lemon–lime combo to the convoluted grape-orange Seven-Up. Fortunately, if they get an upset stomach, the pharmacist is still there to give advice.

Shenandoah

The Sanctuary
207 South Elm, Phone: (712) 246-5766

Situated in a former Christian Science Church and Reading Room, this eatery and coffeehouse is a tasteful discovery for both its ambiance and its gourmet good food.

Scented topiaries of rosemary flank the doorway, and the light coming through the stained glass windows gives the whole room a honeyed, soft aura. Eclectic gift items for sale are displayed artfully throughout.

In this grace-filled light, the Sanctuary serves up some fantastic fare (don't expect to find pork tenderloin or fried chicken here). Sandwiches are put together with made-daily focaccia bread, grilled on a panini grill. Besides the smoked turkey, roasted red pepper, and artichoke combo (lavished with a feta cheese spread), there's also a great turkey, cream cheese, and tomato chutney number. Stop in on a hot summer afternoon, and the soup of the day could be an unusual but tasty chilled cucumber beet soup—pretty in pink, aromatic with dill. Sample that cranberry iced tea too.

Top your meal off with a truly divine dessert. Baked fresh daily, you'll have to choose between such delights as a raspberry cream cheese pie, Sinful Chocolate Cake, cool orange trifle—or on special occasions, creamy tiramisu. The Sanctuary is also the best place in the region to find a steaming and well-made latte or cappuccino.

George Jay Drug
612 W. Sheridan Avenue, Phone: (712) 246-2635

The thing to order here is the strawberry malt. Made with fresh strawberries and buzzed up in the shake maker behind the beauteous cool black marble counter here, they are impressive. Served with the metal container holding the leftovers that didn't fit in the malt glass, they're also like getting two for one!

Sit on one of the black leather-topped stools here and you can admire the ornate gold cash register (the computerized version is next to it), as well as the traditional drinking-straw-holder on the counter. Besides the mirrors, the wall behind holds dozens of snapshots of kids who have enjoyed ice cream here

For years, ice cream cones and kids have been part of the scene at the George Jay Drugstore in Shenandoah.

through the years. According to locals, they start them out with ice cream in a twenty-five cent "baby cone," and not long after, the kids are showing up as teenagers—ordering Cokes flavored with cherry or vanilla.

This is another drugstore/soda fountain with more than a hundred-year history —and if you were driving through town and didn't look closely, you'd miss the small neon lit sign over the door here boasting "soda fountain." Do make a stop next time through.

Council Bluffs

Pizza King
1101 North Broadway, Phone: (712) 323-4911

The name screams "franchise!" but this place is locally owned and operated. Known more than 35 years for its stone oven pizzas, it looks more like an old-fashioned supper club than a pizza shack. Tables and cushy burgundy booths fill the spacious room, mirrors reflect a huge crystal chandelier, and carpet softens the din.

Steaks, seafood, and sandwiches are on the menu too—and there's no doubt (this being next door to Omaha) that the prime rib offered on Friday and Saturday is top-notch. But the thin crust pizza's still the king here, with more than 15 varieties to choose from and prices ranging from $7.50 for a small pie to less than $15 for a large one. The King Special version comes loaded with sausage, onions, and green peppers; a vegetarian variety is heaped with mushrooms, sauerkraut, broccoli, peppers, and olives.

Dairy Queen Memories

Those looking for DQ nostalgia should stop here at the nation's oldest existing Dairy Queen, 1634 West Broadway. Located just west of the Broadway viaduct, this is the 10th Dairy Queen ever built, and still retains its original ice cream cone sign atop the building.

Duncan's Café
501 S. Main Street, Phone: (712) 328-3360

This vintage family-run restaurant has been a Council Bluffs standby for more than 30 years. Cheery tabletops in different colors (bright yellow, blue, red, purple, and pink) fill the middle of the old, high-ceilinged space while tall-backed dark wood booths (the kind with hooks on the ends for hanging your hat or coat) line the sides. Exposed brick walls plus a black-and-white tiled floor add to the homespun character of the place.

Customers come for a breakfast of thick slices of French toast or chicken-fried steak with eggs and hash browns. Lunchtime, get some of the soup (I love the bean with big chunks of ham) or the daily special, e.g., highly flavored goulash and zesty garlic bread. You also can't go wrong with Duncan's famous home-style pork tenderloin, especially if you order it with mashed potatoes and gravy. When gravy is made the way it should be, there's nothing more comforting, and Duncan's gravy maker obviously knows the secret.

Duncan's isn't the easiest to get to if you're coming off the freeway, but it's worth the time. Do call the place; they're happy to give directions.

Glenwood

Two Sisters and Me
405 Sharp Street, Phone: (712) 527-1111

A funky, artsy coffeehouse on the corner of Glenwood's town square, this colorful place feels more San Francisco than small town. Local art adorns the walls, the espresso machine buzzes all day, and a scone or one of those yummy snickerdoodle cookies (or both!) are perfect accompaniments.

Two Sisters and Me is a sunny place to linger over lunch as well. Fridays, a shrimp bisque is the star, but the tomato roasted garlic soup is excellent too. Add a grilled chicken with provolone on focaccia and life looks good again.

Tip: *If you're in town for the evening, catch a movie over at the old Royal Theatre across the square. It's got the best popcorn in the area.*

Mondamin

Small's Fruit Farm
Phone: (712) 646-2723

Tradition runs deep with apple growers like the Small family. One of Iowa's oldest family-run orchards, it originated when Russ Small's great-grandfather chanced to purchase some apples in 1894 from a local farmer here. Remembering the taste to be unusually good, he returned the following year, purchased the farmer's land, and started planting his first orchard in the heart of the windblown Loess Hills overlooking the Missouri River Valley.

Today you'll find Russ and Joyce Small, along with their son and daughter-in-law, Jim and Renee Small, taking care of the orchard and its daily business. Nearby, Russ's brother Gary Small operates another orchard, Mondamin Fruit Farm.

A Small Family Favorite: Apple Crisp

Simple and easy is the way Joyce Small describes her microwave recipe for this autumn classic.

Fill a 9-inch-square glass baking dish with about 5 cups peeled and sliced apples. Add 1 cup granulated sugar, 3/4 teaspoon cinnamon, pinch of salt, and 1 1/2 tablespoon flour to the apples. Mix well. Soften but do not melt 1/4 cup of butter or margarine. Add 1/2 cup granulated sugar, and 1 cup flour to the melted butter. Mix well until crumbly. Put this mixture on top of the apples. Microwave for a total of 16 minutes—turn a quarter turn every 4 minutes. Serve warm or cold. For added pleasure, add ice cream or whipped cream!

Courtesy of the Small family and reprinted with permission.

Located about three miles east of Mondamin, Small's Fruit Farm has long been a popular stop in the autumn. Bus tours pull over, and families bring the kids out for tractor rides around the 70-acre orchard (the existing older orchards were planted by Russ's father Ellis Small, who spent his lifetime as an apple grower). Out here you can see cider in the making or pick apples from among more than two dozen varieties grown.

If it's a Halloween pumpkin you need, they've got those too. In the Sales Barn, visitors can stock up on jellies, butters, Iowa-grown popcorn, and more. But most folks are more interested in the Pie Parlor—where a slice of not-to-be-missed apple, cherry, or peach pie can be enjoyed along with a sample of apple and/or cherry cider. Those who appreciate this fragrantly good stuff purchase a jug to stash in the cooler for a picnic stop later on.

As for those pies: years ago Joyce started baking pies at night for people who placed orders. Soon demand grew, and it wasn't long before she was making and freezing over a thousand pies a year. These days, the demand exceeds what she can make herself, so with the help of a few able pie bakers they whip up around five thousand 10-inch pies a year—all made from Joyce's recipe and to her strict requirements.

Lenox

Tyler Pharmacy
107 N. Main Street, Phone: (641) 333-2260

Down the street from the public library in the sleepy, quiet town of Lenox is the Tyler Pharmacy. With its Iowa flag flying proudly out front and plenty of

Hawkeye memorabilia displayed within, it's not hard to figure out somebody here is a proud Iowan from way back. As it turns out, this family-owned pharmacy was established in 1880 by Iowan O.D. Tyler, and today only one other family-owned pharmacy in the state exceeds Tyler Pharmacy's 124-year history—that being Penn Drug in Sidney, started in 1863.

Step inside here, and a celadon green counter-topped soda fountain is the first thing you see, with black-topped stools, and a gorgeous antique cash register behind. Boxes of Whitman Sampler chocolates and Russell Stover candies are stacked nearby to sell, and a partial list (17 people!) of those who received their early medical and pharmaceutical training here is on the handout sheet next to the register—to "help our customers get to know us better."

It's obvious this place is a favorite among the young set too (witness the

A soda fountain summertime standby.

kids sitting at the counter), mainly because it only costs a quarter for a phosphate drink. The decision is a tough one, though, with flavors like blue raspberry, lime, vanilla, strawberry, cherry, and grape. You can always combine a few or sample a Zombie (at Tyler this means cherry, strawberry, and vanilla combined) or ask for a Zinger, a sweetly refreshing mix of lime and vanilla. This drugstore is a Pepsi-affiliated one, so you can also get a Pepsi whip if you're flush with cash or skipping the chocolate malt today.

Don't leave without taking at least a quick look at the many pharmaceutical antiques on display, including intriguing stemmed and glass-topped bottles that still look like they're half full of various liquids and powders: camphor, gentian, castor. Another little display case has an old-fashioned scale, banana split ice cream dishes from 1915, and small-bowled ice cream spoons.

Hamburg

Stoner Drug
1105 Main Street, Phone: (712) 382-2551

This is one drugstore where you don't even realize there's a soda fountain within until you make your way back to the corner where the school supplies are

Stoner Drug's soda fountain in Hamburg serves up sundaes and sodas with "more of everything."

A Taste of Scotland in Iowa

Sample Dundee cake and scones, sip tea, and listen to the pipes and drums of Scotland as Mount Ayr celebrates its Scottish heritage with Ayr Days, held the second weekend in September. Located east of Lamoni on Highway 2, Mount Ayr is named after the birthplace of the Scottish poet Robert Burns. Don't leave town without tasting a bridie, a meat and vegetable stuffed pastry that's quite delicious.

Soda Fountain Lingo

The following colorful terms were once commonly used by local soda jerks. Some are unique to a particular soda fountain.

Adam's ale—water

Black Stick—chocolate ice cream cone

Brown Cow—various definitions include a root beer float made with chocolate ice cream instead of vanilla and a float made with cola instead of root beer

Bucket of hail—ice

Dipsy Doodle—phosphate with strawberry, cherry, lemon, vanilla, and orange syrups (Wilton Candy Kitchen)

Float—carbonated drink to which scoops of ice cream have been added

Green River—lemon-lime phosphate

Hadacol—root beer and vanilla (Wilton Candy Kitchen)

House Boat—banana split

Mud—chocolate

Odd Ball—strawberry and vanilla phosphate (Wilton Candy Kitchen)

On Wheels—to go

Phosphate—carbonated water and flavored syrup

Pink Lady—cherry and vanilla phosphate (Reiney's Soda Fountain)

Red River—strawberry and cherry phosphate (Wilton Candy Kitchen)

Soda—flavored syrup mixed with small amounts of ice cream and carbonated water to which larger scoop of ice cream and more carbonated water are added

Strawberry Blonde—strawberry and vanilla phosphate (Reiney's Soda Fountain)

Suicide—phosphate made with all available flavored syrups

Whip—carbonated drink with whipped ice cream

White Cow—vanilla shake

Zinger—lime and vanilla phosphate (Tyler Pharmacy)

Zombie—cherry, vanilla, and strawberry (Tyler Pharmacy)

kept. In fact, you can almost hear the buzz of the malt machine before you see the vintage marble counter and stools.

Originally opened in 1896, Stoner Drug was located three doors north of its present location until 1956. The marble fountain that folks belly up to now for ice cream sodas and sundaes was installed in the 1920s.

Stoner makes its banana splits, sundaes, malts, and shakes using the ubiquitous-to-Iowa Blue Bunny ice cream. There's vanilla, chocolate, strawberry, butter brickle, chocolate chip, and rainbow sherbet. According to the menu, the sodas are "luscious ice cream in a flavored beverage. Our sodas have more of everything—prepared as a soda should be." If you order one here, you'll know they aren't kidding.

If you want to have Stoner's specialty, though, go for something called a Fried Egg Sundae. No, there aren't any eggs in it; it only resembles a fried egg over easy, the waitress will tell you. Basically, it's vanilla ice cream topped by marshmallow cream, edged in a drizzle of chocolate.

Stoner is also one of the few fountains that still serves sandwiches as well. And you cannot—must not—leave here without a carefully made ham salad sandwich. This is real home-style fare, served on your choice of white or wheat bread, toasted or not, with a leaf of iceberg lettuce (just like mom used to make) layered within. If you get it to go, it's wrapped in a waxed-tissue-like paper, along with an icy crisp slice of dill pickle and a bag of chips.

Sidney

Penn Drug
714 Illinois Street, Phone: (712) 374-2513

I can't think of a better place than Penn Drug to learn the art of putting together a perfect chocolate ice cream soda (see sidebar).

Facing Sidney's courthouse square, this historic shop (look for the painting of the large ice cream soda on the window) is the oldest (since 1863) family-run drugstore in Iowa.

Step inside, and the first thing to see is the soda fountain—complete with black marble counter and a half dozen or so spin-around stools. Lists above entice with syrups and toppings, from banana, black raspberry, and butterscotch, to strawberry and vanilla. "The orange syrup isn't as good as it used to be," states the clerk. "And the prettiest soda has to be the lime one."

Whatever you order here will be good, that's for sure, and made expertly. If you go for a shake or malt, do know that they'll be too thick for a straw. Only want a scoop of ice cream? At sixty cents a scoop (ninety-five cents for two) how can you deny yourself?

This is another of the few soda fountains left that serve up sandwiches. And if I thought their ham salad was fabulous, I was informed by the woman next to me (sipping her chocolate soda) that on Mondays the egg salad sandwiches are even better.

Penn Drug in Sidney is the oldest (since 1863) family-run drugstore and soda fountain in the state.

The back of the store is where the pharmacy is, and on the wall above the greeting cards, perfumes, and makeup, you can see the drugstore as it appeared years ago-in black-and-white photos. "See that toaster in the photo?" one of the soda fountain girls points out. "This is the same exact toaster, and it's still working," she shows me behind the counter.

It's safe to say not much has changed in this drugstore. It's a gem.

How To Make a Chocolate Ice Cream Soda the Penn Drug Way

First, take a soda glass, pour in chocolate syrup (measure three fingers sideways on glass for correct amount). Add a small spoonful of vanilla ice cream (unless it's a double chocolate soda, then you add chocolate ice cream). Work the syrup and ice cream together until it's all incorporated. Then add fizzy water to it, another scoop of ice cream, and top it off with a bit more fizzy water. Stick in a straw and a long handled spoon. Voila, the perfect chocolate ice cream soda.

My thanks to the girls from Penn Drug who took the time on a hot Iowa afternoon to explain and demonstrate the proper way to make this great concoction.

Mike Whye's 10 Iowa Food Favorites

Mike Whye is a freelance writer, photographer, and author of *Great Iowa Weekend Adventures* and *The Great Iowa Touring Book*, both published by Trails Books. He has also written numerous articles on Iowa for a variety of publications.

Ox Yoke Inn, Amana. German style food—great entrees served with side dishes that never end because the waitresses keep refilling the bowls of vegetables, mashed potatoes, and so on if you empty them.

The Drake, Burlington. Located in what appears to be a former warehouse near the Mississippi River, this restaurant opened in 2003 and already has quite a name. Menu includes well-done sandwiches, pasta, salads, and some entrees featuring elk raised on a nearby farm.

Florencia Mexican Grill, Arnolds Park. A few years after I fell in love with the food from the southern Mexican state of Oaxaca, our family was visiting Arnolds Park—and happened into this Mexican grill whose owner is from Oaxaca. You can order off a menu, or do the buffet: Mexican style vegetables and potatoes, shredded beef for tacos, mild and hot pork, beef and chicken and more.

Living History Farms, Urbandale. In the wintertime, a fantastic restaurant opens when the Living History Farms sets upsuppers in the farmhouse of its 1900 Farm (one of several historical farms on the grounds). Food is cooked in wood—fired ovens and stoves, and served steaming hot to the table that seats ten people. (I felt like I was in a Norman Rockwell painting come to life—my friends and I even played the pump organ for a while.) Some of the best-ever old-fashioned meals I've had have been at the "farm." But forget the diet or cholesterol here; this is one of those meals you're just going to have to bend the rules and enjoy.

Wilton Candy Kitchen, Wilton. I can hardly pass Exit 271 on I-80 without pulling into Wilton for a stop at this ice cream shop, which has been in business since before 1920. Owners George and Thelma Nopoulos make their own ice cream and their own sauces—and when various berries are in season, they get them locally to put in and on the ice cream. Can you ask for more?

World Pork Expo, Des Moines. This annual, three-day event in Des Moines may be arranged for those in the pork industry (lots of exhibits on feeds, equipment, and so on) but if you're interested in sampling some of the best meals featuring pork that you'll ever have, this is the place. From 11 a.m. to 2 p.m. each day, cooks from across the nation prepare pork in all sorts of delicious ways.

El Patio, Des Moines. Anytime I plan a trip to Des Moines, I devise a way to stop at El Patio for lunch or supper. It's located in a nice, large former home, with lots of small, intimate dining areas—even a small outside patio.

Hickory Park, Ames. Serves some of the best barbeque dishes and best desserts you'll ever have.

Happy Joe, numerous locations throughout the state. It may be a chain, but I think it makes the best taco pizza anywhere.

Duncan's Café, Council Bluffs. In an older building, Duncan's has been the place to eat in downtown CB. Luncheon specials are posted daily, the open-faced sandwiches are great, and you're given a plentiful amount of whatever it is you order. Even though my cholesterol count says I shouldn't, I indulge in the hash browns two or three times a year. Service is great, but don''t expect the waiter or waitress to lay a check on your table—it will be waiting at the cash register when you leave.

Central Region
Corn on the Cob and Blue Cheese

In truth, if you never left Interstate 35, which pretty much slices the state of Iowa vertically in half, you would no doubt think that Iowa is basically a flat, albeit fertile farmland, with cornfields and soybeans filling acre after acre after acre—and the capital city of Des Moines plopped smack-dab in the middle of it all.

But exit off on some of the state's smaller highways and byways, and you're in for scenic (and delicious) surprises in this midsection of the state. In the fall, you can find picturesque apple orchards—always tasty stops for a late September treat. How about a slice of homemade apple pie or a warm apple dumpling drenched in sweet cream?

If you're near Fort Dodge's Community Orchard, you might want to simply pick up a bag of apples and a jug of fresh cider and head down to Dolliver Memorial State Park for an impromptu picnic. The park is a pretty little secret just a few miles south of Fort Dodge. The Des Moines River and Prairie Creek wander through here, and there are bluffs and small canyons, even Indian burial mounds—along with sheltered picnic areas.

Near Jefferson, the family-owned Deal's Orchard is a little more off the beaten path, but it's an absolutely delightful autumn destination, especially during their fall festival when fiddle music fills the farmyard, apple cider is being freshly pressed, and hayrides to the pumpkin patch are popular.

Marshalltown, a half-hour drive east off of Interstate 35 (on Highway 30) boasts the Appleberry Farm, with its share of apples, pumpkins, and autumn delights. Marshalltown is also home to all sorts of great eateries worth the drive; from the homespun Stone's Restaurant (where the Mile-High Lemon Chiffon Pie is the star) to the newest Tremont's Italian Grille downtown—conveniently located across from Lillie Mae Chocolates. If you're looking for something truly unusual to do here, check out the unique 12-level tree house built in a maple tree. It features music, sound effects, and even a spiral staircase! Located at historic Shady Oaks Campground—a Lincoln Highway landmark—you can also see a restored tourist cabin that once served travelers on this historic highway.

Ames is home to one of the most beautiful college campuses in the nation, and if you drive next door to Boone, you can hop aboard the Boone and Scenic Valley Railroad for a dinner ride through the lovely Des Moines River Valley.

Who hasn't heard of the world-famous Maytag appliances? Near Newton, you'll also find the family's other claim to fame—their Maytag Blue Cheese. Take a spin out to their Dairy Farms, and you can pick up some of the creamy, rich wheels, along with rounds of the white cheddar cheese that they make here as well.

Dutch specialties await in Pella. Whether you travel to their annual spring Tulip Festival or not, this Central Iowa town is fun to visit—a touch of the Netherlands in the heartland. Dutch architecture, a canal, windmills, wooden shoes, chocolates, and almond-infused pastries are all here.

There are even vineyards in Iowa's midsection. Stop at Summerset Inn and Winery near Indianola and see for yourself. Owner Ron Mark founded this vineyard in 1989, and today it's one of the few wineries in Iowa specializing in wine made from grapes grown in their own vineyards. Besides a beautiful tasting room and shop, this is a lovely place to spend the night. (The Marks offer two rooms and two suites, along with breakfast in the morning.)

If you're looking for a place to picnic, the bridges around Madison County make a fun detour. Stop in to the Madison County Welcome Center in Winterset first, though, to get your map listing the locations of all the bridges in the surrounding countryside. Of course, if you're an aficionado of Robert James Waller's novel, you'll want to check out the Roseman Bridge—where Francesca left a note inviting Robert to dinner. (Be aware: There's even a gift shop nearby now.)

Perry is another central-Iowan small town with some big surprises. Take a peek into the beautifully renovated Hotel Pattee—with its lobby decorated in the Arts and Crafts style—and some absolutely spectacular original artwork exhibited throughout. More than 70 artists, many from Iowa, have their works displayed in this AAA 4 Diamond hotel. Across the street, the town's Carnegie Library has been restored to its original appearance inside and out. In the main Reading Room you can see the first thousand books that were purchased in 1904 for the library—along with a collection of the best sellers and award-winning books from the middle of the 19th century to the present. Throughout, there are displays and exhibits. Certainly, it's a "library about libraries"—but best of all, it's also a library that you can use. Many volumes in the collection may be borrowed by cardholders. Afterwards, you can stop for a cup of coffee and a slice of rich chocolate layer cake at the Victorian-inspired and lace-curtained Thymes Remembered tearoom in town.

When it's corn season, roadside stands are everywhere in Iowa.

So sure, if you're looking for the next fast food franchise or chain motel, stay on the freeway. But if you're searching for some authentic hometown flavors—a summer night concert in a small town Courthouse Square, an all-you-can-eat corn feed, apples from a family orchard, or a slice of mile-high lemon chiffon pie—take the next exit. You won't be disappointed that you did.

Jefferson

Deal's Orchard
1102 244th Street, Phone: (515) 386-8279

On an autumn Saturday, do not pass through this region without a visit to the Deals' apple orchard. It's not the easiest to find (when was the last time you drove a quarter mile on gravel?) but the drive is well worth it.

The farm offers a good selection of apples—more than 25 varieties are grown here, including Cortland, Chenanego, Connell Red, Snow, Winesap, and Honeycrisp. You can pick your own or buy them already bagged up. The Deals also make and sell their own fresh apple cider. If you're lucky, you may be here on a day when they crank up the cider press (in the fall, two or three times a week). Watching and then tasting the cold, freshly pressed juice, has to be one of best autumn experiences there is. The Deals bottle over 35,000 gallons of this aromatic and wonderful juice.

The sales barn is filled with all sorts of other goodies—bags of locally grown popcorn, jars of honey and jam, kitchen gadgets, and caramel apples.

The second weekend in October is their annual Fall Festival—a fun and friendly affair. There are horse-drawn hayrides to the pumpkin patch and all sorts of activities for the family: corn-shelling, candle-dipping, rope-making, a corn maze, and even a pumpkin ring toss. Fiddle music fills the farmyard and folks wander everywhere, visiting with friends or sitting at picnic tables—digging into warm pastries oozing apples and cinnamon, in between spoonfuls of ice cream. If you can't be here then, know that the fab apple dumplings and pies that people are sampling are always available for sale in the shop's freezer case—and they bake up at home real nice. Trust me on this one.

A family orchard started more than 80 years ago by Frank Deal, today the orchard is owned and operated by Frank's grandson Jerald and his wife Cindy along with their three sons. Their enthusiasm for the fall season still shows.

Tone Brothers, Inc.
Located in Ankeny, Tone Brothers, Inc. was founded in Des Moines in 1873. Today, it is the second-largest manufacturer of herbs and

spices in North America. Here's a recipe for a rich apple cake featuring Tone's Cinnamon Maple Sprinkle.

Cinnamon Maple Sprinkle Apple Cake

2 cups sugar

2 cups flour

2 teaspoons baking soda

$1/2$ teaspoon salt

2 teaspoons ground cinnamon

2 eggs, beaten

2 teaspoons vanilla extract

4 cups finely chopped, peeled, cored, apples

$1/2$ cup vegetable oil

$1/2$ cup brown sugar

1 tablespoon Tone's Cinnamon Maple Sprinkle

Caramel Topping

$1/2$ cup butter or margarine

$1/2$ cup brown sugar

$1/2$ cup sugar

$2/3$ cup evaporated milk

1 tablespoon Tone's Cinnamon Maple Sprinkle

Cake directions: Preheat oven to 350 degrees.Combine sugar, flour, baking soda, salt, and cinnamon in a large mixing bowl. In a separate mixing bowl, combine eggs, vanilla, apples, and oil. Add mixture to the dry ingredients and stir just until well mixed. Batter will be thick.

Pour cake batter into a greased 9x13 pan. Sprinkle with brown sugar and cinnamon maple sprinkle.

Bake 50 to 60 minutes, or until a toothpick inserted in center comes out clean.

Caramel topping directions: Combine butter, sugars, and evaporated milk in medium saucepan on medium heat. Stir constantly, bring to a boil for 1 minute. Add cinnamon maple sprinkle. Cool.

Cut cake and serve with caramel sauce. If desired, top with ice cream or whipped topping.

Recipe courtesy of Tone Brothers, Inc. and reprinted with permission.

Marshalltown

Lillie Mae Chocolates

23 West Main Street, Phone: (641) 752-6041;
(800) 752-6041

There is nothing like the seductive, buttery smell of homemade caramel, and during the fall there's nothing like crisp Iowa-grown apples dipped in the stuff—especially if it's the caramel apples at Lillie Mae's.

The season for caramel apples is never long enough, but even if you miss it here, know that anytime you stop in the shop you're going to find wonderful delights. In the mornings, when Georgia Dates is usually dipping chocolates at the marble top (in view of customers), the smells of melting chocolate are a timeless pleasure—and it's fun to watch the process. After she dips the fondants, she gives a twirl with her thumb to initialize each cream: pineapple, butter, cherry, toffee—each one gets its special swirl.

During the fall, there's nothing like one of Aimee Snyder's caramel apples from Lillie Mae Chocolates in Marshalltown.

This is also one of those great little hometown sweet shops with a history. Since 1939, Lillie Mae's has been providing Marshalltown residents with their chocolate Easter eggs, Valentine candy, Christmas treats—and caramels, nut clusters, and everything else in between. Today's candy boxes feature a lily, but

49

originally the boxes had a likeness of a little girl—Lillie Mae—named for first owner George Demopolus's young daughter.

Since that time, the store has been relocated twice (this is its third location), and for many years it was operated as a candy shop and café. In 1992, owners Buck and Georgia Dates (Georgia's parents, Andy and Helen, owned the shop for many years) remodeled and expanded the candy operation here—enlarging the main floor area so that visitors could watch the chocolates being hand-dipped.

In 2003, the shop was sold to Marshalltown natives Aimee and Tom Snyder, but Georgia remains an integral part of the store—hand-dipping chocolates, stirring up the caramel, and teaching Aimee all she can to help carry on the traditions of Lillie Mae Chocolates.

Stone's Restaurant
507 South Third Avenue, Phone: (641) 753-3626

Mile-High Lemon Chiffon Pie (it actually angles nine inches to the peak) is what it's all about at Stone's, an eatery and Marshalltown institution since 1887. The famous pie has been part of its history since the early 1920s, when the recipe was said to have come to Anna Stone in a dream, and "we've never been told otherwise," says current owner and Anna's grandson Randy Stone.

This is the second oldest continually run, family-owned restaurant in the state ("it's seven years younger than Breitbach's," says Stone, referring to the long-established restaurant north of Dubuque). Randy Stone's great-grandfather, Esbon, started the business in 1887 selling sandwiches and coffee. In 1909, he purchased the hotel, bar room, and pool hall across the street, and

Sample the famous "Mile High" lemon chiffon pie at Stone's restaurant in Marshalltown.

Stone's has occupied this building ever since.

"Under the viaduct, down by the vinegar works" is printed on the paper placemats that Stone's Restaurant uses today. The slogan was developed by George Stone and wife Anna to help auto travelers on the old Lincoln Highway find the restaurant. Although the pickle factory is long gone, folks traveling today over Marshalltown's Third Avenue viaduct will catch sight of the last neon sign on Highway 14, which sits atop Stone's Restaurant. You do indeed still need to pass under the viaduct to find this place.

Not much has changed inside, and that's part of its charm. The old wood display cases, the counter, and spin-around stools remain in the front room. In the dining room Abraham Lincoln's bust still sits, surrounded by dark ceiling beams. There's also a portrait of Anna Stone, considered the guiding force in getting lace tablecloths on the tables and fresh flowers in the room, whose attention to the quality and detail of food and service attracted not only crowds from the local area, but some famous folks of the times. Since then, stories about Stone's have appeared in *National Geographic, Saturday Evening Post,* and *Gourmet.*

Still, if you come to Stone's only for the pie, you're missing out. The food here is hearty, homespun, and good. You won't find iceberg lettuce at the salad

Stone's Mile-High Lemon Chiffon Pie

In the 1920s, Anna Stone taught Queenie Weir, a young pastry chef at the time, to make this pie. Queenie continued to work at Stone's until she was in her 70s and then baked out of her home. Today, Stone's baker, Jeannette Eggers, makes the restaurant's daily allotment of lemon chiffon pies. When she began baking the pies years ago, her instructions from the retiring baker were short and sweet: "This is how you do it. And I'm not going to show you again." (She didn't.) Luckily, Eggers caught on. In 2001, *Gourmet* magazine rated the treat one of the country's top 10 pies.

Tip: For best results when making this recipe, choose a cool day with low humidity.

8 egg yolks, slightly beaten

1 cup sugar

2 lemons (juice)

2 lemon rinds, grated

salt to taste

2 tablespoons unflavored gelatin

1/2 cup cold water

8 egg whites, beaten

1 cup sugar

Cook first five ingredients in double boiler, stirring frequently, until consistency of thick custard. Set aside to cool.

Soak gelatin in cold water until dissolved—add to hot custard and cool.

Beat egg whites stiff but not dry. Beat in sugar gradually and then beat again. Fold cooled custard into beaten egg whites. Put in baked pie shell and chill three hours. Serve with whipped cream.

Recipe courtesy of Randy Stone and reprinted with permission.

bar; you will find mixed greens, five kinds of macaroni salad, two kinds of potato salad, pickled herring, and even a glass pan of red Jell-O. Lunch and dinner entrees include stalwart Midwestern standards like hot beef sandwiches, tender beef hearts, chicken casserole, and scalloped potatoes and ham. But a fifth generation Stone in the kitchen (Randy and Judy's son Joe) is updating the menus with more seafood and salads.

When it's time for dessert at Stone's, of course, who can resist that sky-high pie? No one. The girls waiting tables even have a contest, says Randy, to see who can carry the most plates of pie to diners. So far, the record is seven plates of pie delivered to a table, all slices still standing—at their quivering nine inches of height. Once at the table, though, it's up to the diner to figure out how they're going to tackle this sweet beast.

Tremont's Italian Grille
28 West Main Street, Phone (641) 754-9082

Home of Muddy Waters Coffee Company, this is the place downtown where you can get a latte and omelet for breakfast, come back for a burger or Jennifer's famous chicken salad sandwich for lunch, and return at dinnertime for pasta.

Next door to their upscale Tremont on Main restaurant, this understated beauty is J.P. and Jennifer Howard's newest venture. A casual stylish décor matches the easy relaxed vibe that pervades the place. The food is terrific.

Sandwiches include hearty choices like the standard half-pound burger or the meatball sub, but don't overlook that grilled chicken fragrant with pesto, piled with greens, red onion, and tomatoes and served on focaccia. Or order something more innovative like Apple Smack on sourdough: smoked turkey, sliced Granny Smith apples, cheddar cheese, and apple butter. How about an Olive Walnut sandwich? The menu does a nice job mixing down-home food with a little city pizzazz.

If it's pasta you're craving, you've come to the right place: the best lunch item on the menu could be the spaghetti with marinara sauce, Italian sausage, and peppers. It's hot; it's spicy. It's totally rich in pure, wonderful flavor. This is no spaghetti sauce from a jar. Don't like spicy? Get the fork-tender chicken parmesan. It's a winner too.

And if it's romance and fine dining you're desiring, don't miss having dinner next door at J.P. and Jennifer's Tremont on Main. Thursday nights there's live jazz; the setting is classy with gilded mirrors and a grand piano, the wine list well-chosen (it's inexpensive too). And the food? More than terrific. Smoked Gouda chicken, orange peel duckling, sesame-encrusted ahi tuna, ginger and lime Florida grouper. The chef here knows what he's doing, does it well, and it shows.

Cecil's Café
13 Iowa Avenue East, Highways 14 and 30
Phone: (641) 753-9796

Just look for the giant chicken with the top hat, and you'll know you're close to Cecil's. This is where the locals eat—a classic homespun old-time café that's been a local favorite for more than 40 years. From five in the morning through suppertime it serves up traditional Midwestern grub, made by somebody in the kitchen who cares what they're dishing up, be it the pancakes and bacon, cinnamon rolls, perfectly cooked eggs, or the burgers and mashed potatoes. The place is clean. It's friendly. It's inexpensive. It's independent. It's what used to be before chains and franchises sprung up by the freeway ramps. Make sure you stop.

Taylor's Maid-Rite Sandwich Shop
106 South Third Avenue, Phone: (641) 753-9684

Nothing but a simple town sandwich shop, Taylor's Maid-Rite is recognized as the oldest of the one hundred Maid-Rite establishments. I'd have to add it could also be the best place to eat one of these ubiquitous-to-Iowa loosemeat sandwiches.

Part of the reason is due to the fact that at Taylor's the 100% prime beef from Iowa gets ground daily here in the basement of this shop—a fact the staff and manager Don Taylor Short (great-grandson of the original owner, Clifford Taylor) are rightfully proud of. This is the good stuff, stirred and cooked to its crumbly (never clumpy) perfection in front of diners sitting at the counter. After the meat is loaded into a soft bun, it's served with mustard, pickles, or chopped onions, wrapped in its logoed tissue and delivered to you. (Some fans don't even bother with the bun and simply order a "bowl of meat.")

The other part of the reason that Taylor's ranks right up there at the top of the best-places-to-eat-a-loosemeat-sandwich chart, is because at Taylor's they make their own ice cream and homemade pies. And really, there's nothing like a Maid-Rite, along with an excellent buzzed-up hot fudge shake (you get the tin that the leftovers are in here too) and pie for dessert.

This is the kind of place where bankers sit on stools across from farmers, moms and pops bring their kids on Saturdays, and grandkids stop in after school to see their grandma—who may be working that day. It's true, not only is the Taylor's clientele loyal, but so is the staff—some have been here for more than 40 years.

Hamburger Shop History

When Clifford Taylor bought his 1928 Maid-Rite franchise in Marshalltown, it cost him $300, according to the brief history that current owner Don Short has written up. The Taylors baked the pies at home, sliced whole pickles from Marshall Vinegar Works, and got their burger buns from Strand's Bakery. When he died, his son Don took over, running the business in the same fashion—even building a cooler in his basement to grind fresh hamburger daily. In 1958, Don built the current building that Taylor's occupies—totally state-of-the-art at the time, with stainless steel, counters up on legs for cleaning, and two cash registers.

Ames

Hickory Park Restaurant
1404 South Duff Avenue, Phone: (515) 232-8940

What started as a small-enterprising little barbeque joint in 1970 is now a huge, sprawling and still-popular place with a parking lot to match. Throngs of Iowa State University fans have been gathering at Hickory Park before and after any athletic competition since the place opened in its first location.

The façade has a faux Western look and there's a front porch area with benches to wait (you can just about always expect a line and a wait, no matter when you're here) or you can sit inside on church pews, taking in the ambiance and terrific aromas. If you're in a hurry, you can opt for the take-out stand right behind the lady taking names for seating.

All things barbecued is the name of the game here, and pigging out is still the tradition. Large beef ribs, pork sandwiches, smoked chicken, and Hickorys—burgers piled with all sorts of toppings—are all good choices. Still, most diners opt for those small and tender pork baby back beauties: luscious, succulent, and slip-off-the-bone tender.

The meat is accompanied by hefty sides of the classics—coleslaw, barbecue beans, potato salad—or homespun choices like buttered corn, mashed potatoes and gravy, hot cinnamon spiced applesauce, three-bean salad . . . the list goes on. It's all good.

After you've polished off your meal, there's more. Dessert here is half the fun. Sundaes include cherry-fudge (topped with a chocolate-covered cherry), or a Merry Go Round (it's topped with animal crackers). There are Bake Shop sundaes: scoops of ice cream plopped on top of pound cakes and brownies, with numerous flavors and syrups and goo to go with. Pretty parfaits, floats and frappes, shakes and malts—this is decision making at its toughest.

Café Beaudelaire
2504 Lincoln Way, Phone: (515) 292-7429

Close to the ISU campus, this little Brazilian café captures the warm and inviting spirit of that South American country. The bar is cool (the top laminated with maps of the world), the tables filled with an eclectic mix of clientele. Near the windows, there's people-watching aplenty in this university neighborhood.

You can come in the morning for espresso and a muffin, or lunch on a heart-of-artichoke salad and seasoned black bean stew topped with a *couve à mineira* (a warm mixture of chopped kale with sautéed onion, garlic, and tomatoes). Late afternoon, stop in for a refreshing (and potent) *cachaça*-based *caipirinha* and a basket of the wedge-cut Brazilian fries—hot, soft insides, crispy skins outside. Served with a dollop of mayo, these are totally addictive morsels. Or try the Cheese Pastels (if they're not sold out). These are handmade little treats, sort of like empanadas.

At dinner there's *beau feijoada*, Brazil's most popular dish according to the menu, a pork steak served over rice with sweet Italian sausage, bacon, and the sautéed kale mixture, then topped with the rich and flavorful cooked-for-hours black bean stew.

During the school season, evenings are often filled with music and special drink deals—one of the most popular being their Friday-night Long Island iced tea tradition.

Newton

Maytag Dairy Farms
2282 E. 8th Street North,
Phone: (641) 792-1133; (800) 247-2458

Made from sweet and fresh Holstein milk, the first wheels of Maytag Blue were formed and put to age in caves in October 1941. Since then, not much has

Near Newton, Iowa's famous Maytag Blue Cheese is produced.

changed, although the Holsteins in the field are long gone (the milk today is purchased from area Iowa farmers). Today, each wheel is still made by hand and aged in caves twice as long as other blue cheeses.

Besides this handmade attention, the extra aging is part of what makes Iowa's Maytag Blue so special, giving it the creamy, rich mellowness and distinct flavor that people around the world have grown to appreciate.

Today, Maytag Dairy Farms are in the third and fourth generations of the Maytag family. If you're interested in visiting, the office and cheese shop are open to the public and welcome visitors. While you're here, you can purchase fresh wheels of blue cheese as well as rounds of their white cheddar cheese (also made at the farms).

Aged nearly a year, the white cheddar has a nice, full-bodied taste and is delicious too. If you're really interested in seeing the cheese-making process, the store also offers a 10-minute informative video showing the history and significance of Maytag Blue Cheese.

Three Fast and Fine Maytag Blue Cheese Recipes

Marge's Maytag Blue Cheese Spread

This is a favorite of the office workers at the Maytag Dairy Farms.

12 ounces Maytag Blue Cheese

8 ounces Maytag White Cheddar

4 ounces cream cheese

Shred Maytag white cheddar, place in mixing bowl, and microwave until melted. Crumble Maytag Blue Cheese and add to white cheddar along with cream cheese. Microwave until soft. Using mixer, mix until smooth for 2 to 3 minutes. Pour mixture into container and refrigerate. When ready to use, microwave a few seconds and stir until of spreading consistency. Serve on crackers, vegetables, steak, or as desired. Makes $1^1/2$ cups. Keeps several days in the refrigerator.

Blue Cheese Quiche

1 unbaked 8-inch pie shell

3 ounces crumbled Maytag Blue Cheese

2 3-ounce packages cream cheese

3 tablespoons milk

1 tablespoon chopped chives

2 eggs

Bake pastry shell in very hot oven, 450 degrees—or according to package directions. Cool. Reduce oven to 325 degrees. Have cheeses at room temperature. Add milk and chives. Beat with electric mixer until light and fluffy. Add eggs one at a time, beating after each. Pour into pastry shell. Bake at 325 degrees for 30 minutes or until almost set. To serve for brunch or lunch: cool 15 minutes; cut in 8 wedges. For appetizer: Chill thoroughly. Cut in 12 wedges. Arrange on a serving tray.

Gene's Maytag Blue Cheese and Asparagus

Another office favorite, this recipe was sent to Maytag Dairy Farms by Gene Witte of Saint Charles, Iowa.

1 pound asparagus spears, trimmed

3 ounces Maytag Blue Cheese, crumbled

3 tablespoons butter, melted

1/2 cup croutons

1 1/2 cup water

In a large skillet, bring water to a boil. Add asparagus; cover and boil for 2 to 3 minutes or until crisp-tender. Melt 3 tablespoons of butter and pour into a large shallow baking dish. Place asparagus in melted butter (should be a thin layer), top with crumbled blue cheese and sprinkle croutons on top of the blue cheese.

Bake in preheated 350-degree oven for 8 to 10 minutes or until cheese is melted.

Recipes courtesy of Maytag Dairy Farms and reprinted with permission.

Grinnell

Carroll's Pumpkin Farm
244 400th Avenue, Phone: (641) 236-7043
Open seasonally

In the fall, a stop at Carroll's Pumpkin Farm is a tradition. Area school kids have been visiting for years on field trips, and it's truly a pumpkin paradise. Pumpkins are everywhere—huge 30-pounders and tiny windowsill ones. There's even a pumpkin tree. Pumpkin-head mannequins sit on bales of hay in front of the sales barn, dressed in overalls and Hawkeye sweatshirts, and everybody likes having their pictures taken with the group.

In the spacious country store, you'll find jars of pumpkin butter and recipes for pumpkin pie made from scratch (there's a novel thought), pumpkin cookbooks, and packages of pumpkin bread mix. There's dumpling squash and patty pan squash for sale, plus all manner of gift-y things. Outside, a small concession stand serves up autumn standbys like popcorn, cider, and caramel apples. Kids love the corn maze. On weekends there are unlimited hayrides and shows in the barn loft. There's even an area for picnicking—or with advance notice you can build a bonfire and roast marshmallows.

Pella

Ulrich's Meat Market
715 Franklin Place, Phone: (641) 628-2771

A spotless little meat market, aromatic and always busy, Ulrich's has prepared its famous hickory-smoked beef bologna "since 1868 from the original recipe of John Ulrich," according to the label on the rings of bologna sold here.

Once you taste this smoky, spicy bologna, you'll never be able to look at the flat flavorless rounds sold in supermarkets quite the same way again. The shop also sells thin-sliced dried beef, summer sausage, brats (jalapeno, pineapple, beer, bacon, and cheddar), beef jerky sticks, double-smoked hams, smoked pork chops, hand-breaded tenderloins, and a whole lot more. Plenty of imported and domestic cheeses (e.g., Gouda, Edam, Komijenkaas) to choose from as well. If you're looking for picnic fixings, they'll slice up some salami for you or even make up a bologna or ham salad from-scratch sandwich. They also have homemade potato salad.

Bologna History

In the display window in the front of the shop, you can read about the maker of the original ring bologna that became known as Ulrich's Pella Bologna. John Ulrich (1847-1930) brought his recipe to America in 1867, making it in Pella by 1868. He made his first bologna by hand, using two small choppers and smoking the meat in barrels. Until he could afford his own butcher shop, it was said that he sold it from a basket he carried around town. By 1884, he was considered one of the best-rated merchants in the city. In the meat market window, there's also a photo of John (who folks said whistled merrily while he made his bologna), and an old bologna-making machine.

Since 1902, the building at 715 Franklin has carried the name of Ulrich's Meat Market.

Jaarsma Bakery
727 Franklin Street, Phone: (641) 628-2940

Founded in 1899, this busy bakery has been making its sweetly famous Dutch Letters with the recipes Herman Jaarsma brought over here as an immigrant from Holland. Back then, though, the Dutch Letters were only made as a special treat for Sinterklaas Day (the Dutch Santa Claus Day), December 6th. If

Sweet Dutch treats on display in Pella.

you've always wondered why "S" is the only letter that you usually see the pastry shaped into, the reason apparently is because it stood for Sinterklaas.

Besides the Dutch Letters (puff pastry wrapped around moist almond paste filling), the bakery also makes the Dutch spice cookies called Speculaas. Originally made in wooden molds and given to children on St. Nicholas' Day, they make them year-round here. Crispy and scented with cinnamon, nutmeg, and cloves, the cookies are still imprinted with a traditional Dutch design—and you won't be able to eat just one. (Tip: They go great with a cup of strong coffee.)

Small and large almond butter cakes are another specialty, and the smaller-size round makes perfect picnic fare for two. Thick and dense, with sugar sprinkles and sliced almonds on top, they're quite decadent. But not as decadent as something else they make: the Beehive. This sinful sugar rush is chocolate cake filled with buttercream, blanketed over with thick chocolate frosting.

Jaarsma also puts out the standard bakery fare, including mini poppy seed bundt cakes, traditional cookies, bars, and angel food cakes. Part of the bakeshop display area is devoted to blue-and-white Dutch delftware, along with books and all sorts of other little gifts sure to please your Dutch auntie.

Van Veen Chocolates
621 Franklin Street
Phone: (641) 628-4222; (888) 822-5225

A sublime little shop that smells divinely of chocolate, this business came about when owner Chuck Van Veen was working in the farm equipment business and giving away samples of his mother's peanut brittle. The candy became so popular that Chuck's mother finally told him she couldn't keep up and he would have to start making his own. Happily, Chuck took his mother's advice, and the Van Veen family's secret recipes were passed on. Now you can purchase the buttery peanut brittle, as well as chocolates and more at this friendly chocolate store.

Picnicking in Pella

Between the bakeries, meat markets, and chocolate shops, picnicking in Pella is almost a given. Happily, Pella has lots of parks to choose from for an alfresco feast.

Big Rock Park (west end of Big Rock Road)

Brinkhoff Park (Highway 163)

Brook Circle Park (Brook Circle Drive)

Caldwell Park (Highway 163)

Central Park (downtown square)

Jaycee Park (North Broadway)

Kiwanis Park (Orchard Drive)

Lions Park (Idaho Drive)

Rotary Park (East 3rd Street)

South Park (South Main Street)

Sunken Gardens Park (Main Street)

Volksweg Trailhead Park (University Street)

West Market Park (Franklin Street)

Vander Ploeg Bakery
711 Franklin Street, Phone: (641) 628-2293

Sure, you can get ultra almond-y rich Dutch Letters here, but don't overlook all the other goodies you might want to try. The white walnut bars are chewy and moist. Dutch Hankies are little packages of raspberry encased in pastry. Breads are many and tasty: rye, sunflower seed, Vienna. Pastry-filled puff pillows are stuffed with Bavarian cream. There are peanut butter cookies and truffle cookies and those always-popular cinnamon crispies. Of course, you can also find the regular bakery repertoire of glazed doughnuts and sweet rolls filled with raspberry, pineapple, butter, and cinnamon.

Folks come from all over the world to visit this charming bakery, grandparents bring grandkids to show where they once bought Dutch Letters for a quarter, and tourists crowd in to see what all the fuss is about. It's all here in this tidy, old-fashioned bakeshop, along with a history that goes back more than a hundred years.

Adel

Sweet Corn Festival
Held the second Saturday of August

You can't miss the town of Adel when its corn festival is going on—the oversize blown-up corn on the cob on the edge of town is a dead giveaway. In town, there's music plus food stands set up all around Adel's historic square. Do take some time to walk around and admire this pretty little town. But don't wait too long before heading over to the tent where the free corn on the cob (more than seven tons!) is being plated up. Get in line for your own portion of the hot, buttery stuff—all you can eat. Then find yourself an empty spot at one of the picnic tables under the tents and squeeze in.

More than seven tons of sweet corn are consumed at the Sweet Corn Festival in Adel.

Picnicking in Bridges Country

Long before the blockbuster novel was written, the real bridges of Madison County were a tourism attraction (but scarcely on the scale they are now). Originally, there were 19 covered bridges built in the county between 1855 and 1885; they were covered to help preserve their large flooring timbers. Today, five of these picturesque covered bridges remain, all listed on the National Register of Historic Places (a sixth was recently destroyed by fire and is being rebuilt). While touring the area, you might want to plan a picnic lunch at one of the pretty sites. One good place for an alfresco outing is near the gracefully arched stone bridge in the charming little Winterset City Park; it's just south of the Cutler-Donahoe covered bridge, and is the same park where Francesca and Robert Kincaid (played by Meryl Streep and Clint Eastwood) go for their getaway picnic in the 1995 movie.

If you want to immerse yourself even more in the movie, you should also head on over to the Northside Café in Winterset, where

Robert dined (at the counter, the fourth stool from the door is the one that was used by Clint in the movie). The café has actually been a Winterset institution since 1876, the food is not bad, and the waitresses might even share some stories about the filming of the movie.

Iowa's Original Apple

Iowans' favorite apple may be the Jonathan, but it's the Delicious apple that owes its existence to a nineteenth-century Iowa farmer named Jess Hiatt.

Around 1870, the story goes, Hiatt started an orchard in Madison County. Not long after, a tree from a chance seedling began growing outside one of his established rows. Hiatt cut it down. The next year, it grew back. He cut it down again. When it appeared again the next spring, he let the persistent sapling stay, and 10 years later it bore fruit. Hiatt dubbed the fruit Hawkeye, but at a fruit competition in 1893, a judge tasted it and called it, "delicious." As it turned out, the judge was the president of the Missouri-based Stark Nurseries, and the next year, Hiatt sold the propagating right to the company.

Perry

David's Milwaukee Diner
Located in the Hotel Pattee, 1112 Willis Avenue

Dedicated to celebrating the luxury train dining experience (check out the luggage racks above the booths), David's Milwaukee Diner even has guests entering through a sleek and silver sliding train door.

It's low-key casual with elegant undertones, and it feels right—welcoming to both the home folk and the traveler on his way somewhere else. This is a small-town hotel restaurant exactly as it was meant to be.

The menu is as brilliant, with one side featuring pricier, globally contemporary cuisine such as Asian crab terrine, roasted pepper duck breast, and poached lobster, and the other side showcasing a less expensive hometown dinner menu: Iowa stir-fry over mashed potatoes, grilled pork medallions with macaroni and cheese.

No matter which side of the menu you order from, you can be assured executive chef Shad Kirton incorporates seasonal produce and local bounty into the recipes. You can also expect outstanding platefuls: robust, rich, and rustic sauces in that Iowa stir fry, pork medallions that melt in the mouth, and mac and cheese that is quite simply homespun bliss.

Desserts are made by another Perry local, Heather Fredericksen. Be prepared. Everything sounds wonderful: banana cream pie, Chocolate Implosion Cake, vanilla crème brûlée. But if it's in season and on the menu, get the rhubarb pie. You won't regret it.

Check out the cozy library in the totally renovated, historic Hotel Pattee in Perry.

A Food-Friendly Place to Stay

Hotel Pattee
1112 Willis Avenue
Phone: (515) 465-3511

Thanks to Perry native Roberta Green Ahmanson, who never forgot her roots, this 1913 brick beauty has been completely renovated. In 1993, it was a run-down shell of a building, depressing and bordering on hopeless. Today, the four-star boutique hotel is a testament to Ahmanson's belief that Perry's heritage and history are valuable and worth preserving. She and her California financier husband Howard put $10 million into the rebuilding of this piece of Perry history.

They didn't skimp. Step inside and natural elegance pervades. This is quality with all the trimmings. The Arts and Crafts era has been retained, starting with the lobby's massive stone fireplace and mahogany paneling. Add the brown leather furniture, Persian carpets, terra cotta tile floor, period chandeliers. There's a gorgeous cozy library with a wood-burning copper fireplace (you can take books, videos, and CDs to your room if you prefer.) And artwork. More than 70 artists, many from Iowa, are represented in the Pattee's collection, displayed throughout the hotel.

Guestrooms each have a story to tell; 34 rooms and six suites reflect the heritage of the city of Perry and the state of Iowa: quilting, marching bands, salutes to farm life, notable locals, immigrants, and even one in honor of Louis Armstrong—Hotel Pattee's most famous guest. All are carried out in detail—fabrics, wall coverings, furniture, lamps, antiques, and paintings. There's even a menu of pillow choices at this hotel, plus modern spa facilities, and—perhaps most fun of all—a two-lane bowling alley.

This is definitely a hotel you want to settle in for a couple days. Linger in the library. Stroll around admiring the artwork. Have a drink in the Inter-Urban Lounge. Eat at David's Milwaukee Diner.

Oh, and go bowling. When the Hotel Pattee opened in 1913, it offered the latest in fitness and recreation—a bowling alley. Today, the modern lanes offer state-of-the-art equipment in a 1913 setting. The lanes are named after Roberta Ahmanson's grandfather, a champion bowler in the 1920s and 1930s.

Thymes Remembered Tea Room
1020 Otley Avenue, Phone: (515) 465-2631

Something sweet comes to mind when you step into the Thymes Remembered Tea Room. Maybe it has to do with the chintz and lace curtains, or pretty-in-pink colors, or details like the little porcelain pitcher that your cream comes in.

More probably though, it has to do with the desserts this place is renowned for: creamy, dreamy, homespun rice pudding with a jewel-toned raspberry sauce topping it. Turtle cake, dense with chocolate filling and caramel, slathered in fudge frosting. Homemade apple pie, warm with ice cream all melt-y, drizzled in caramel and pecans. Need I go on?

For the past 11 years, this inviting tearoom has been serving up some of the best Midwestern desserts in the state. These are hearty classics—the kinds of things your grandmother might have made prepared (if she was a really good baker), made with farm-fresh ingredients and served with love.

But the tearoom isn't just about desserts. Their lunches are excellent as well.

The menu changes weekly, and every day there are five entrees to choose from. Try a slice of velvety quiche—maybe asparagus and ham and cream—served with a fine little salad of greens dressed in their signature Vidalia onion dressing. (You can buy bottles of the dressing in the Calico Shops adjacent to the tearoom.) Or try the tearoom's traditional chicken salad (theirs is fruited with pineapple and oranges, touched with a hint of curry dressing). Their Kitchen Sink Salad is another popular choice—loaded with greens, bacon, smoked turkey, baby sweet peas, cran-raisins, and more, it's a flavor-packed entrée that even guys find filling. (Yes, the boys are welcome at this tearoom too.) Soups are homemade: thick and cheesy vegetable for winter or a refreshing and cool strawberry concoction that's a summer standby.

The tearoom is not open for breakfast—but on Saturdays a brunch is always served at 9:30. (You'll need reservations.)

The Thymes Tea Room's Chilled Strawberry Soup

2 cups frozen strawberries, thawed

2 cups sour cream

Blend together until smooth. Season to taste with confectioner's sugar and a little almond extract. Serve chilled, with a couple sliced strawberries to garnish, and a dollop of whipped cream on top.

This keeps several days in the refrigerator. Serves 4.

Recipe courtesy of Thymes Remembered Tea Room and reprinted with permission

Webster City

Raspberry Festival
Held on the weekend before the Fourth of July

Okay, first of all, you need to know that there are no huge raspberry patches surrounding Webster City. Not that a couple small patches of the precious little jewel couldn't be found, of course. But the real reason for this fun small-town festival (begun in 1998) had more to do with simply choosing something to celebrate to bring the community together. So why not raspberries?

Taking place at the 7-B Ranch, it's a day to remember. Start with raspberry pancakes at the requisite pancake breakfast—and make plans to get here early if you want to be assured a plateful.

At 10 a.m. the construction of HyVee's annual largest raspberry dessert begins. This is always fun to watch. Every year there's a different dessert constructed. One year it was a 16-foot diameter raspberry pie. Another year it was a huge chocolate raspberry sundae, and still another was a raspberry cheesecake. Once the sweet confection has been put together, more fun ensues. Everybody gets to eat it.

As much as they want. Free.

The event also has its requisite craft fair; there's always stage entertainment, horseshoe-throwing contests, and, of course, a recipe contest. The recipe contest is a small one (only 20 adult and 10 juvenile entries are allowed) and the raspberry recipes don't need to be original. But they do need to contain at least one cup of raspberries, says Loween Clayberg, the event's coordinator. There are plenty of prizes too, including gift certificates to many local businesses. In the kids' division this means places like Dairy Queen, the town theater, and the local bowling alley. In the adult division, besides cash and gift certificates, this is the only recipe contest I know of where second prize includes half a hog, processed.

After lunch, there are plenty of amusements for the kids, or you can wander through 7-B's well-kept gardens and ponds. In the evening there's usually a musical show put on in the tent where the pancake breakfast took place.

When darkness finally falls, dig out the old army blanket from the trunk of your car and stake out a place on the huge lawn. Then stretch out and watch some of the most amazingly awesome fireworks you'll ever see at a small-town gathering.

Raspberry Ribbon Pie

In 2004, Emily Hackman, age 10, won first place in the juvenile division of Webster City's Raspberry Festival for this rich and wonderful pie. When her younger brother saw all the goodies and prizes she won, he decided he will be entering the recipe contest when he's eligible.

1 1/4 cups graham cracker crumbs

1/4 cup sugar

6 tablespoons butter, melted

1 3-ounce package raspberry Jell-O

1/4 cup sugar

1 1/4 cups boiling water

1 12-ounce package frozen red raspberries

1 teaspoon lemon juice

1 8-ounce package cream cheese, softened

3/4 cup powdered sugar

1 teaspoon vanilla

Dash of salt

1 8-ounce container Cool Whip

Pie Crust: In a mixing bowl, combine crumbs and sugar. Stir in melted butter; toss to thoroughly combine. Turn the crumb mixture into a 9-inch pie plate. Spread the crumb mixture evenly into the pie plate. Press onto the bottom and sides to form a firm, even crust. Chill about 1 hour or until firm.

Red Layer: Dissolve Jell-O and sugar in the boiling water. Add frozen red raspberries and lemon juice; stir until berries thaw. Chill until partially set.

White Layer: Meanwhile, blend well the cream cheese, powdered sugar, vanilla, and salt. Fold in a small amount of whipped cream, and then fold in remainder. Spread half of the white cheese mixture over the bottom of pie shell. Cover with half the red Jell-o mixture. Repeat layers. Chill until set. Garnish.

Recipe courtesy of Emily Hackman and reprinted with permission.

Stanhope

Stanhope Locker
465 Parker Street, Phone: (515) 826-3280

Located 13 miles south of Webster City, the small town of Stanhope is home to 450 people, Country Relics Village, an antique shop, and this renowned little meat locker.

Bring your cooler when you visit because you'll want to stock up on any number of wonderful meats that are available here. The locker has its own smokehouses and considers its specialty to be its spiced beef jerky, but its summer sausage, beef sticks, cottage bacon, bologna, dried beef, and smoked hams are all worthy—and delicious too.

Along with more than two dozen beef cuts, they have more than 40 pork cuts available: in the pork chop division alone, you can choose from center chops, Iowa chops, loin center chops, American chops, butterfly chops, stuffed chops, and smoked chops. In addition, there are roasts, ribs, sausages, and even Cajun pork patties and a Luau Loaf.

A Food-Friendly Place to Stay

Hook's Point Country Inn
3495 Hook's Point Drive, Stratford
Phone: (515) 838-2781

"We've had people come here for the stars," says Mary Jo Johnson, who along with her husband Marvin, owns Hook's Point Country Inn. Indeed. This country-quiet 1904 farmstead, located about one mile north of Stratford, is far, far away from city lights—and if you've never seen a star-studded night in the country, this is the place to be dazzled.

For several years, the couple also dazzled guests with multi-course home-cooked meals: tenderloin of beef smoked over grape wood, corn bread and honey butter, desserts like homemade vanilla ice cream. *Bon Appetit* magazine heard about them, and came out and did a story. Things got crazier, and busier. Finally, the two decided it was time to slow down, and stopped the dinner-making altogether.

That's the bad news. The good news is that you can still spend a night or two in a feather bed here, see the stars, wander around a real working farm, and enjoy breakfast at their morning-bright dining room table. The coffee is served in a silver coffee pot, there are antique goblets filled with yogurt, topped with fresh strawberries, plus sliced melon on a platter. There's French toast and scrambled eggs with chives from the garden. Afterward, you can sit out on the porch with a cup of coffee, watch the birds, read a book, or simply listen to the quiet.

Hook's Point Crusty Corn Bread

"Through the years, I've tried many recipes for corn bread, and this one is the best," says Mary Jo Johnson of Hook's Point Country Inn. It has more sugar than most recipes, which makes it crustier. It was contributed to the Stanhope, Iowa, Christian Church Cookbook printed in the 1950s, says Mary Jo. A neighbor of hers told her she had found the recipe on a corn meal box in the 1930s.

If you have a #5 or #6 cast iron skillet, or if you have a clay bake dish, you will find the corn bread is even crustier and will stay warm longer for serving.

Dry mixture

1 cup flour

1 cup corn meal

4 teaspoons baking powder

$1/2$ teaspoon salt

Liquid mixture

$1/2$ cup sugar

2 eggs

1 cup milk

Reserve 3 tablespoons of melted butter.

Slightly beat eggs, add sugar, then milk. Stir this into the dry mixture. Stir in the melted butter. Pour into a greased pan, 8x8, or a warmed cast iron skillet. Bake at 400 to 425 degrees for about 20 minutes.

Prepare ahead tip: Mix up several recipes of the dry mixture to put in individual plastic bags. You can be ready on short notice to serve hot corn bread.

Mary Jo's Honey Butter

1 part honey to 3 parts butter. (You may like yours sweeter, says Mary Jo.) One stick of butter should be about right for one recipe of corn bread.

Using an electric mixer, whip the butter until it is very pale yellow. Slowly drizzle in the honey while continuing to mix.

Recipe courtesy of Mary Jo Johnson and reprinted with permission.

Diana McMillen's 10 Iowa Food Favorites

Diana McMillen is the food editor for *Midwest Living* magazine in Des Moines.

Paradise Pizza Café, West Des Moines. They have a wonderful Sunday brunch. Their regular menu is great too, with fun pizzas (my fave is the California pizza), great pastas, and a boysenberry soda I just love.

Zanzibars coffee shop, Des Moines.

New Pioneer Co-op, Iowa City and Coralville.

La Mie Bakery and Restaurant, Des Moines.

Classic Frozen Custard, West Des Moines. Cotton candy frozen custard is our favorite, along with lemon and coffee.

Waterfront Seafood Market, West Des Moines.

Palmer's Deli has three locations, soon to be four, in the Des Moines metro Area. They do everything right. Brownies to die for, wonderful sandwiches (including some creative combinations) and restaurants that are clean, bright, and co temporary. Yum.

La Corsette, Newton.

Aunt Maude's, Ames.

Lincoln Café, Mount Vernon. A small, bistro-like eatery. The menu changes daily.

Des Moines

Supper Clubs, Cinnamon Rolls, and the State Fair

From its well-established supper clubs to its newest sushi bars, Des Moines is a blend of old-fashioned country with big-city sophistication. Its gold-domed capitol building alludes to its history. The Principal Financial Group building points to its future. A bona fide city in every way, including a freeway constantly under construction, its rural roots still run deep (who hasn't heard of its famous state fair?).

Summer Saturdays in the historic Court Avenue district, you'll find the bustling farmers' market, with more flavors of the farm, as vendors set up stands offering warm-from-the-oven cinnamon rolls, truckloads of fresh corn on the cob, angel food cakes, and strawberry jam. Locals and tourists alike crowd the streets purchasing homegrown tomatoes and rhubarb, or bright sunflowers for their kitchen tables—then take time to dash into Java Joe's for a quick espresso.

If you're in this area toward evening, you might want to duck downstairs for an early dinner at The Trattoria, a cozy gem tucked away on Court Avenue. Order any of its daily specials—although you may want to stick with the caramelized onion linguine with artichokes and garlic in white wine sauce if it's being featured. The expanding area is also now home to an authentic British pub: Check out the Royal Mile for fish and chips, or the Hessen Haus for a cold stein of German beer, a bratwurst, and oompah music.

Farther downtown Des Moines, a different vibe ensues. In the original Masonic temple, there's the hip Centro—a happening place (serving incredible pizza) in a great restored building. Not far away (and next to the Hotel Fort Des Moines) is the Raccoon River Brewing Company; this is where you want to order the beer cheese soup and the platter sampler of beers for a fun tasting. Raccoon River is one of several brewpubs in Des Moines; Court Avenue Brewing Company and Granite City Food & Brewery in Clive are two others worth a visit.

Those looking for steakhouses in DM won't be disappointed at 801 Steak and Chop House, a topnotch (and top-priced) place with prime people watching—especially when all the political gurus hang out here during caucuses. Jesse's Embers is an Iowa tradition—an affordable treasure that's been around for more than 40 years.

Seafood and sushi aficionados can be appeased in the capital city too. Try Splash Seafood Bar and Grill at Third and Locust, Arirang Restaurant, or Taki Japanese Steakhouse —which features not only sushi, but also personable chefs who do individual tableside cooking.

Fiery-food lovers in the city will adore the popular Thai Flavors. Des Moines also boasts a selection of Mexican and Latin American specialties—don't miss a shopping trip to La Tapatia Tienda Mexicana market for all kinds of discoveries. At the other end of the dining spectrum, Younkers Tea Room downtown is nice if you're in the mood for a walk down memory lane—or taking your great-aunt out to lunch.

On Ingersoll Avenue, four of my fave Iowa stops are all within a few blocks of each other: coffee at Zanzibar's Coffee Adventure, a Manhattan (as in the sandwich here) at Manhattan Deli, Bauder Pharmacy for ice cream, and Chocolaterie Stam for outstanding chocolates and gelato.

Italian food has always been a big part of Des Moines' culinary landscape. There's everything from the newest Basil Prosperi in the skywalk downtown to the tried-and-true Tursi's Latin King Restaurant (yes, it's Italian—go figure). Gino's family restaurant has long been known for its famous salad dressing and its Italian fried chicken. Baratta's boasts excellent calamari and manicotti—and don't forget its cannoli for dessert. Noah's Ark Ristorante is one of the oldest locally-owned Italian restaurants, and besides the antipasti, lasagna, and homemade rolls, it makes some of the city's best and most-beloved pizza.

Plenty of dining options can be found outside of the downtown area too: In West Des Moines, Palmer's Deli & Market puts together superb sandwiches, and for fresh seafood you can't beat the Waterfront Seafood Market.

In historic Valley Junction, you can find decent dim sum at Café Su, and its fortune cookies come dipped in chocolate!

Urbandale is home to the Iowa Machine Shed Restaurant—and one of the biggest, best pork chops around. The restaurant is also a must-stop for anyone who has never seen farm equipment, never worn overalls, and doesn't know what you're talking about when you mention seed hats. Of course, if it's romance and fine dining you're wanting, the place to make a reservation in this suburb is at Trostel's Greenbriar.

However, on a hot summer Saturday night when you're just looking for a bit of nostalgia, head over to the city's George the Chili King Drive-Inn. This is the night you're usually assured of seeing plenty of shined-up restored vehicles parked in the lot. Cruise on in to join the crowd, and don't leave without an order of George's onion rings.

La Mie Bakery and Restaurant
841 42nd Street, Phone: (515) 255-1625

What's not to love about this classy, spotless shop offering a stunning assortment of French pastries that are as beautiful to behold as to eat? Rum-soaked, sugar-glazed, fruit-filled, buttery-rich, oozing smooth pastry cream, the enchanting offerings are vast. The breads are nothing to be passed over, either. And this doesn't even take into account the lunches or dinners or Sunday brunches!

Located in a strip mall called the Shops at Roosevelt, La Mie hardly seems the mall type, but it does make a nicely sophisticated match for the cool, upscale stores here. Muted lavenders and grays plus black accents, with framed artwork on the walls, infuse the long and slender space with an elegant ambiance. Private booths and tables in back get filled quickly, especially on Sunday mornings (the only day breakfast is served).

The only dilemma here is deciding what to order, because you'll want to taste it all. Sunday mornings, there's the ham and brie French Pizzetta—a marvel of puff pastry layered with smoky ham, creamy brie, scallions, and a scattering of cured olives that gives it just the right savory kiss. Another winner: tender crepes filled with custard and apricots. But wait, there's more: A wedge of mile-high creamy quiche. And more: The cinnamon-encrusted French toast. Most morning entrees include a little sauce bowl of fresh yogurt, dribbled with dried cranberries, walnuts, pistachios, and sliced strawberries.

At lunchtime, sample the fine Salad Nicoise with fresh tuna, or the buttery grilled Croque Monsieur. At dinnertime, look for the pork loin. No matter how it's prepared, it'll be outstanding—like everything served here.

The thing you've got to remember, though, is that at La Mie the menu changes frequently, so it's important not to get your heart set on a certain something. Then again, you need never really worry too much, because no matter what you end up with, I assure you, it won't disappoint.

The Shops at Roosevelt, founded in 1931, is the oldest shopping center in Iowa.

Java Joe's Coffeehouse
214 4th Street, Phone: (515) 288-5282

A sense of history and timeless energy pervades this coffeehouse that I find irresistible. Maybe its allure has something to do with the daily rich scents of coffee beans roasting and wafting out over the sidewalk here in the capital city's historic Court Avenue district. Or maybe it has something to do with the building it's housed in that dates to 1875, with interior brick walls and kitschy coffee antiques. Whatever it is, I can't make a trip to Des Moines without a stop for a cappuccino or espresso at Java Joe's.

Baked goods, breakfasts, and sandwiches are all offered here—and at night there's live musical entertainment and even some open mic nights and poetry slams. The place thrives with clientele of all ages, and the spirit is coolly casual, citified, and, like the coffee it serves, just plain addictive.

Graziano Brothers, Inc.
1601 South Union Street, Phone: (515) 277-7103

In a quiet and sleepy little neighborhood, this Italian grocery store is the kind you don't see much anymore. Once you're near here, you can't miss the two-story red-painted brick building with the sign Graziano Bros, Est. 1912 painted on the side. (But getting here can be a problem.) Still, once you've found the place, you'll remember it—and return.

The store is small by the warehouse grocery store standards of today, but plenty big enough to offer a remarkable selection of Italian goods. Aisles are loaded with jars of Pomi tomato sauce, a huge selection of risotto, bags of bulk pasta, and bottles of olive oils—and rich with the scents of bulk herbs and spices. Bread from South Union Bread Company fills another corner display. The freezers hold tortellini, ravioli, and pizza crusts. There are boxes of those Balocco Italian cookie wafers and Baci biscotti.

For history buffs, it's interesting to take a look at one of the back walls where black-and-white photos of the place show the way it was—and the people who worked here then; there are even huge, framed castle-like keys that were brought from the homeland. Shelves nearby are stacked with imported pasta makers, ravioli cutters, platters, and bowls from Italy. Near the front of the store, they even have the Italian stomach relaxer Brioschi.

But best of all has to be the cheese and meat counter in the rear of the store. Here's where you buy Parmigiano Reggiano, *prosciutto* di Parma, gorgonzola dolce, ricotta salta, fresh mozzarella, Graziano's fragrantly seasoned olives, plus cylinders of house-made salami and strings of well-spiced sausage—either the smoked or garlic version is highly recommended.

Des Moines Farmers' Market
Court Avenue and Fourth Street, Phone: (515) 243-6625

When you're walking the block or so over from the Savery Hotel, you hear the downtown Des Moines Farmers' Market before you see it. Music wafts along the street just ahead of mingling market aromas: apples, fresh flowers, cinnamon rolls, herbs. It may be 7 a.m., but "It's never too early for the blues," according to these street musicians.

This is my kind of Farmers' Market—not too big, not too small, with a little bit of everything, including live music. Since 1974, Des Moines residents (and tourists in town as well) have been heading to this cluttered, colorful market located in the historic Court Avenue District of downtown Des Moines. Encompassing several blocks, it's open from Mother's Day weekend in May through Halloween, 7 a.m. to noon every Saturday.

With the streets closed to traffic, everybody wanders along the sidewalks, admiring Iowa peaches "picked last night" according to the hand-printed sign in front of them. Baskets of jumbo green peppers and sun-warm tomatoes are set up at stands next to displays of handcrafted jewelry that sparkle enticingly. Across the street, whimsically painted birdhouses are lined up on the top of a parked van.

At this Midwest market, it stands to reason that warm, soft cinnamon rolls lavished with frosting are offered for sale at several places, along with croissants stuffed with chocolate, and light-as-a-cloud angel food cakes—frosted or plain.

If it's mid-July or later, find the backs of pickups filled with melons—and signs stating these aren't just any melons, but Muscatine melons. Some sellers' signs even go so far as to boast (and rightfully so) "grown in my garden by me." Ripened under a hot Iowa sun and harvested on a sandy piece of soil in southeast Iowa, the Muscatine melon really is something special. Meltingly sweet and succulent, it's just plain sensuous on the tongue.

In August, of course, there's corn for sale everywhere. It's also loaded in the back of pickup trucks. Homemade signs advertise Peaches and Cream or

On summer Saturdays in Des Moines's historic Court Avenue district, you'll find the bustling Farmer's Market.

Candy Corn varieties—the names are as sweet as the corn on the cob itself.

Then again, don't overlook that other corn—the salty sweet confection indigenous to the Midwest: kettle corn. Made with Iowa popcorn, it's popped in a huge copper kettle set up under a canopy and heated over a gas-powered flame. While the kettle corn maker stirs it all with an enormous wooden spoon, you can watch as it's sprinkled with sugar, forming each piece of the popcorn's signature crackly-like-thin-ice shell. Then it's all salted, bagged up, and set out for sale. It's a must-buy.

For some of the best goat cheese in the state, check out the Northern Prairie Chévre (see sidebar) where fine quality artisan cheese is made from the milk of "well-loved goats." There's always cheese for sampling, and while doing so, you'll no doubt hear tidbits about how people are using the chévre in their recipes—for example: fill crepes with lemon-zested chévre, roll up, pour over with some fresh blueberry coulis, top with Chantilly cream and Cointreau. (That's one I just had to write down.)

At another little stand, baby food jars filled with homemade lemon chutney are displayed while fresh warm potato cutlets are made on the spot, scenting the air with exotic spices. Down the block you can pick up a bun piled high with pulled pork.

Need a bag of fortune cookies or egg rolls? Bouquets of sunflowers with happy faces on them? Eggs? Home-crafted root beer? Keep walking and keep exploring, because you'll find all this and more at the Des Moines Farmers' Market, an essential experience for all genuine food lovers.

A Place for Gourmet Cheese

Northern Prairie Chévre
1247 310th Street
Phone: (515) 438-4022

When Wendy Mickle and Kathy Larson brought home two adorable little Nubian goats, who knew that the animals would eventually be the commencement of a successful cheese-making venture?

Certainly not Mickle or Larson. They bought the bred does with the intention of selling the kids to 4-H children. But as the kids grew both Mickle and Larson became attached and couldn't sell them. Eventually the two-goat family grew into quite a herd. So did milk production. Not knowing what to do with all that milk, the two turned to friend Connie Lawrance, who was enthused about cheese-making. And the rest, as they say, is history.

Today, the three turn out approximately 250 pounds of cheese per week, all from Kathy and Wendy's six-acre farm near Woodward, Iowa. Their brand, Northern Prairie Chévre, comes in a variety of flavors, as well as French Style Feta, Caprine

Farmhouse, Marinated Caprine Farmhouse, Queso Blanco, cheddar, Manchego, and Parmesan. All of them bear a fresh flavor and smooth texture that is attributed to the farm's particular breed of goat, Nubian. The cheese can be ordered online at www.northernprairiechevre.com (The women also make and sell decadent, rich hot fudge sauce from the goat's milk).

A Couple of Recipes from Northern Prairie Chévre

The following are two favorites of the owners.

Smothered Chops

6 center cut pork chops, breaded and fried

1 can cream of mushroom soup

4 ounces garlic-flavored chévre

Combine soup with chévre and heat until steamy to make sauce. Pour over chops on a bed of rice or pasta.

Vidalia Onion Risotto with Feta Cheese

2 teaspoons vegetable oil

2 cups chopped Vidalia onion

2 large garlic cloves, minced

$1^1/2$ cups Arborio or other short-grain rice

2 cans, 14.5 ounces each, vegetable broth

$1/2$ cup crumbled feta, divided

$1/3$ cup chopped fresh parsley

$1/4$ cup grated Caprine Farmhouse cheese

Freshly ground pepper

Heat oil in saucepan over medium heat. Add onion and garlic and sauté one minute. Stir in rice.

Add $1/2$ cup broth; cook until liquid is nearly absorbed, stirring constantly until each portion of broth is nearly absorbed before adding the next.

Remove from heat; stir in $1/4$ cup feta, parsley and

Caprine Farmhouse cheese. Spoon rice mixture into serving bowl. Top with remaining feta and pepper.
Recipes reprinted with permission.

A Food-Friendly Place to Stay

Renaissance Savery Hotel
401 Locust Street
Phone: (800) 798-2151; (515) 244-2151

Guests can't help but be impressed when they walk into the lobby of this historic 1919 hotel. Marble floor, butter yellow walls surrounding a sparkling chandelier—dripping elegance over a circular "gossip" settee—a stunning area rug specially made in Europe. Best of all, despite the opulent look of the place, it still manages to feel friendly and welcoming.

Listed on the National Register of Historic Places, these rooms have seen such prestigious guests as Woodrow Wilson, Harry S. Truman, Eleanor Roosevelt, Jimmy Carter, and Bill Clinton. Located in downtown Des Moines, the hotel is convenient to restaurants, coffeehouses, and just a block or so from the Des Moines Farmers' Market—a summertime must-visit.

At the Renaissance, you can also dine in the Iowa Room, where the bounty of the state gets top billing, with specialties such as pork tenderloin, Maytag Blue Cheese corn bread, and classic bread pudding.

Kirkwood Corner Coffee Shop
400 Walnut Street, Phone: (515) 244-9191

Located in the historic Court Avenue District, this is the quintessential corner coffee shop café I grew up on. I can still envision going to these kinds of places with my dad. Sitting on a spin-around stool at some counter, watching my pop stir a bit of sugar and cream in his cup of coffee (and a lot of cream and sugar in mine) while he bantered with the waitresses is a memory hard to beat. At the Kirkwood, it's not a memory. Guys still sit at the counter, guzzle gallons of coffee, and tease the waitresses, who dish it right back at them.

But I don't ever recall being served up a cinnamon roll (except my mom's) like the ones they make here. It's a huge Iowa number—they warm it up and slather it with butter that melts all through it. Untwisting the soft and cinnamon-y coil, savoring that scented, warm sweetness—well, what more can I say? It's a happy way to start the day.

Centro
1011 Locust Street, Phone: (515) 244-7033

This bustling urban eatery with its high ceilings, comfy banquettes, vintage French advertising posters, and open kitchen evokes a welcoming and warm ambiance.

Housed in downtown Des Moines' miraculously restored Temple for the Performing Arts, Centro (pronounced "chen tro") draws in a casually chic crowd. And whether they're converging around tables sharing pizza, sipping glasses of wine, or downing Goose Island beers on tap, they seem to give the place its incredible energy.

As for the food: Locals know never to skip the bread basket here—with South Union Bread Company's George Formaro heading up Centro's kitchen, this bread really is top of the line. (His South Union Bread Company shop is next door, so if you're looking for a quick lunchtime sandwich for the road, this makes a great stop too.)

Centro's menu, a creative mix of classics with an Italian influence, includes appetizers like crab cakes or excellent bruschetta. Entrees such as handmade cavatelli spiked with sausage, or creamy Parmesan-sauced pasta tossed with tender wood-grilled chicken and prosciutto are worthy choices as well.

Still, the favorite has to be their signature brick oven-fired pizza. This is an authentic Neapolitan pie—with a smoky, crisp crust that only a coal-fired brick oven can produce. Sample it with artichokes and ham, or roasted peppers and anchovies; eat it simple Margherita style with only fresh mozzarella, tomato sauce, and basil. Whatever you choose, it's a guaranteed winner.

Centro is a hip urban eatery serving up irresistible pizza in downtown Des Moines.

801 Steak and Chop House
801 Grand Avenue, Phone: (515) 288-6000

If you want to see the opposite of a ladies-who-lunch restaurant, visit the 801. Located in the tallest building in downtown Des Moines, you have to go inside the glass foyer and up a level here to find the place. But from the moment you pull open the 801-shaped brass door handles and catch the drift of men's voices, see the booths filled with well-dressed powers that be (especially during political caucuses: is that Tom Brokaw over there? Ted Kennedy?), then note those huge framed paintings and photographs of . . . yes, mean-looking bulls (real bulls) that hang on the gorgeous dark wood-paneled walls, it's apparent this is a place where serious wheeling and dealing takes place.

The cushy booths are topped with etched glass partitions inscribed with "U.S. Prime" and "801," table linens are thick and luxurious, the bar stretches long and polished, and the bartender makes a magnificent and perfect martini. (Try the Jamaican number if you're not a purist.)

The menu here is demonstrated as the servers show off two-inch-thick Iowa pork chops and raw beef, explaining the various cuts (filet mignon, porterhouse, New York strip, et al.). Sides are served family style, and everything comes in humungous portions (share those Maytag Blue Cheese-sauced spuds). Prices are high, but for such splendid meat and excellent service you won't be disappointed, and you'll understand why this is considered one of Des Moines' top restaurants.

Jesse's Embers
3301 Ingersoll Avenue, Phone: (515) 255-6011

I have to admit, the first time I parked near this stark, white, windowless building on the corner of Ingersoll, I was less than impressed. It hardly looked inviting. But once I stepped into Jesse's original, cozy, dark-paneled eatery, and the scent of sizzling grilled meat wafted over, I was hooked.

Home-owned, owner-operated, Jesse's has been a Des Moines tradition for more than 40 years (it opened in September 1963). Thirty years later, Rich Roush opened the second location in West Des Moines. But it's still the original I prefer returning to.

The space has been described as a sort of *Cheers* setting, and it's easy to understand why. No, it's not that the place necessarily resembles the Cheers institution; it's the fact that the feeling in the place is one of camaraderie and neighborly friendliness. (Even better, this is also the kind of place where the seasoned bartender knows if you want to chat or be left alone.) Yeah, the TV is on in the corner over the bar, but it's not blasting. Guys come in to pick up barbeque ribs to go; waitresses know customers' names. You want to eat at the bar tonight? It's okay. Want to split that Ladies' Steak Sandwich with your sister, honey? No problem. At Jesse's, it's all good.

The menu has chicken and seafood, but most folks are here for the low-priced open-pit steaks or ribs (aged Black Angus beef)—with the Ember Burger and onion rings close seconds. Steaks cut like butter and are seared to juicy perfection. Dessert? How many places have you seen lately that boast old-fashioned ice cream drinks like a Pink Squirrel or a Golden Cadillac? Leave room.

Zanzibar's Coffee Adventure
2723 Ingersoll Avenue, Phone: (515) 244-7694

With over 30 varieties of freshly roasted coffee beans from around the world, Zanzibar's fragrant little shop will lure you inside simply to marvel at the bags of beans available. Just reading the exotic names makes a coffee aficionado get all giddy: Jamaican Blue Mountain, Indian Monsooned Malabar, Zimbabwe, Celebes Kalossi. At the drink counter, besides caps and lattes, Zanzibar's also knows how to blend up a creamy hot chocolate or a rich mocha. In the summertime, sample one of their cool Italian sodas. If you're not sure what you want here, the staff is super friendly and happily offers a taste of anything.

Located on the well-trafficked Ingersoll Avenue, the coffeehouse has been around more than 10 years. It's always a fun stop—especially early in the morning, when you can sample the Eggs Expresso (two steamed eggs with cheese), hide behind the newspaper, and discreetly check out some of the capital city's leaders stopping by for their caffeine fix.

Bauder Pharmacy
3802 Ingersoll Avenue, Phone: (515) 255-1124

Step into the past at the family-owned Bauder Pharmacy. From its pretty, octagon-tiled floor, its soda fountain with bright blue cushioned spin-around counter stools, and old-fashioned prescription center (complete with Schwartz drawers and antique pharmacy bottles of potions displayed atop), the place could almost be a museum.

Except the glass case of roasting nuts up front is fragrantly doing its work, there are pints of freshly made ice cream (lemon custard, coffee, chocolate, strawberry, among about 30 other flavors) in the cooler nearby, and there's usually a handful of teenagers at the counter, sipping strawberry floats through a straw or scooping into a hot fudge sundae made with Bauder's award-winning ice cream.

Let's face it, birthday cards and blood pressure pills aside, it's the homemade ice cream owner Mark Graziano and his sister Kim make in the back room that keeps folks coming back. Summertime, fresh peach and strawberry ice cream sell out fast. At State Fair time, don't miss a visit to their stand for one of their awesome handmade peppermint, fudge, and Oreo ice cream bars. At Christmas time, look for their spumoni ice cream—loaded with pecans and maraschino cherries and all sorts of the good stuff, it's truly special.

Both Mark and Kim are pharmacists as well as the ice cream makers here, and along with their mom ("we couldn't do it without her," says Kim), work hard to make this shop the Iowa culinary treasure it is. Do stop by.

At Bauder's Pharmacy, it's the homemade ice cream that keeps folks coming back.

Chocolaterie Stam
2814 Ingersoll Avenue, Phone: (515) 282-9575

Wandering into this spacious, aromatic shop off busy Ingersoll Avenue in Des Moines feels a little like falling into a chocolate dream. Make that a European chocolate dream. Maybe that has something to do with the sign out front stating: "Amsterdam-Des Moines."

Amsterdam? Indeed. This chocolate operation has its roots in Holland,

Sample the outstanding chocolates and gelato at Chocolaterie Stam in Des Moines.

where the Chocolaterie Stam story originated. The story? In the early 1800s, an ancestor there (Jacobus Stam) ran a bakery whose reputation for chocolates finally encouraged him to specialize in chocolates exclusively. Eventually, three of Jacobus's four sons and one daughter joined their father in the chocolate business. One of them, Frits, had seven sons, and it is his youngest, Ton, who felt that America might appreciate such sensual delights. When Ton's financial planning work brought him to Des Moines in1997, he decided to see if America was ready for these family chocolates. Today (three shops later), he knows they are.

With more than half of the chocolates made on-site, the remainder is flown in biweekly from the Stam's family chocolaterie in Holland. These butterfat-rich chocolates feature close to 45 fillings (some made with créme fraiche, and all covered in custom-blend chocolate. As beautiful to behold (cream caramel is a tiny tower, coconut ganache is shaped like a butterfly) as they are to bite into, these are chocolates you give to chocoholic friends who appreciate and savor such finely crafted treats. Several chocolates simply have the Stam name stamped on them; others have bas-relief illustrations. They are undoubtedly some of the best chocolates (at some of the best prices) I've eaten in the state.

Besides the sweets displayed so temptingly in their shining glass cases, the shop also offers small tables where customers can sip an espresso or indulge in hot chocolate.

Summertime, an adjacent patio with greenery, potted blooms, and lights strung through the trees is an enchanting little oasis to relax in and cool off with a round of perfect, lush lemon gelato. Yes, along with its chocolates, the place also makes its own gelato (10 to 20 flavor variations, depending on the day you visit.)NOTE: Two other shops include one at 6611 University Avenue in Windsor Heights, and one in Valley West Mall in West Des Moines.

Tursi's Latin King Restaurant
2200 Hubbell Avenue, Phone: (515) 266-4466

This cherished neighborhood gem has been an Italian perennial favorite with Des Moines residents since 1947. Get a glimpse of that flashing neon crown and "Fine Food" sign high atop the place, and no doubt you'll expect a retro supper club below to match.

But you'll be wrong. From the parking lot, you can see the outline of the patio with its big pots of flowers. Step inside the door from this little terrace, and Italian wine country visions come to mind. Softly hued Tuscan villa colors pervade, and the feeling is one of upscale sophistication, with linens and cranberry shaded lamps shedding a romantic little glow. Yes, the Latin King updated its look a few years back, redoing its menu too, according to loyal patrons. But it's all been for the better, they say—keeping the best of the past (big platefuls of spaghetti and meatballs, house-made ravioli) with some fresh new tastings.

Even so, I'm still partial to the old house specialty of Chicken *Spiedini*—marinated hunks of chicken breasts, lightly breaded and grilled, then served in a lemony-garlic olive oil. I also like their antipasto plate (especially those white beans with fresh rosemary and garlic). And if you haven't already managed to taste the Des Moines tradition known as Steak Du Burgo yet, the Latin King is where you should do so.

Governor Tom Vilsack's 10 Iowa Food Favorites

A special thank-you to Governor Vilsack for providing the following list of 10 of his favorite Iowa restaurants—noting also that they are in no particular order of preference.

Tursi's Latin King Restaurant, Des Moines

Noah's Ark Ristorante, Des Moines

Palms Supper Club, Fort Madison

Hamburg Inn Number 2, Iowa City

Mario's Italian Restaurant and Lounge, Dubuque

Baratta's Restaurant and Pizzarea, Des Moines

Mount Hamill Tap, Mount Hamill

Jonesey's, Solon

Jersey's Pizza, Mount Pleasant

Waterfront Seafood Market, West Des Moines

Metro Market
2002 Woodland Avenue, (515) 288-1121

With more than 30 vendors, this indoor year-round market is the Des Moines version of the great public markets of Baltimore and Philadelphia. Located at the corner of Martin Luther King Parkway and Woodland Avenue, the plain building doesn't look like much from the outside, but when the snow is swirling and wind is howling, nobody much cares about the exterior. It's what inside here that counts.

The building is open Friday and Saturday, from 9 a.m. to 7 p.m., and that's when you'll find friendly sellers handing out free samples and recipes—along with showcasing their culinary specialties for sale. For road trippers, this is a great place to stock up on picnic supplies, get a taste of some of the state's best products, or have a bargain meal; after purchasing and picking up your food from any number of stands, you simply mosey on over to the communal and spacious area where tables are set up for diners to eat.

Mornings, get your caffeine fix at **Kinkajou Coffee**, select a cinnamon roll from the **Flour Shoppe**, or nibble on one of those rich almond Dutch Letters from the **Vander Ploeg Bakery** stand (of Pella, Iowa fame).

Buy a jar of honey from **Log Chain Apiary** (it's collected from the meadows near Allerton, Iowa) and make sure you stop at the **Picket Fence Creamery** stand (out of Woodward, Iowa) early if you want a brick of their absolutely

Find Italian cuisine and specialties at Café di Scala in Des Moines's indoor Metro Market, where more than 30 vendors from around the state offer their culinary best to shoppers.

incredible and fresh creamery butter. Picket Fence also sells premium ice cream like apple cinnamon and cherry vanilla, and white cheddar cheese curds. If you've never tasted real farm-fresh milk, this is the place for a sample. (PFC offers Grade A Creamline, a term meaning non-homogenized-milk; it's 100 percent natural, free of artificial hormones, antibiotics, and chemicals.) This is the way milk is meant to taste.

At the **One Stop Meat Market**, there's a great selection of everything from buffalo burgers to rib eyes, Iowa pork chops, and spiral cut hams. Another stand sells elk. At **Lynch BBQ**, besides ribs and roasts and barbequed pork sandwiches, they also sell seasonings and sauces. (Note: Lynch's Country Market is also located at 4900 Merle Hay Road, a quarter mile south of Interstate 80, in the Sinclair service station; hot barbeque available from 10:30 a.m.!)

Lunch or dinner time, check out **Rosario's Mexican Kitchen** or **The Greek Menu**, where Toula Ballou dishes up gyros and handmade pastichio (the Greek version of lasagna).

At **Café Di Scala** you can find imported Italian specialties like olive oils, as well as proprietor Anthony Lemmo's made-from-scratch meat and vegetable lasagnas and raviolis (check the freezer case). Don't overlook jars of his spicy fresh marinara, house-bottled garlic vinaigrette, or packages of traditional Italian sweets like guantis and loveknots, made by Lemmo's mother.

Breads and focaccia arrive warm from the ovens at South Union Bread Company here too, and there's a nice selection of Italian wine. Basically, this is the best place to find all the fixin's for a perfect and stress-free Italian feast at home (without messing up your kitchen.).

But Café Di Scala is also a favorite with locals for lunch, offering an assortment of first-class sandwiches made with TLC. Whether you sample Frank's Special—slices of toasted garlic focaccia layered with basil pesto, fried eggplant, grilled red onions, marinated tomatoes, and provolone cheese—or you opt for the flavorsome but simple eggplant Parmesan sandwich, you won't be disappointed.

Smitty's Tenderloin Shop
1401 Army Post Road, Phone: (515) 287-4742

Since 1952, Smitty's has been serving up the King Tenderloin, a pounded-thin, crisply fried, big as a plate-sized-pancake piece of pork. This is the "home of the REAL whopper" a cartoon on the wall states—and when you see the hunk of meat with a tiny token bun atop, you'll get the idea.

A nondescript shack south of Des Moines (near the airport), Smitty's is always busy—with people dining in at the few booths, sitting at the counter, or driving up and hopping out of trucks to pick up bags of the steaming hot tenderloins to take home. If you taste only one tenderloin in Iowa, taste this one.

George the Chili King Drive-Inn
5722 Hickman Road, Phone: (515) 277-9433

A summer Saturday night in Des Moines means a stop at this classic drivein. Don't bother looking for speakers to order from—the car-hops will show up at your car window (they're watching from inside the little eatery). When you've chowed down your Coney dog and are ready to leave, simply blink your headlights or drive up to the window.

George's has been a DM institution for more than 40 years and is well known for its burgers and chili. Indeed, both are worthy, properly greasy— and delicious. My advice is to tack on an order (or two) of the onion rings here as well. These circles of wispily battered onion are hot, tasty, and totally irresistible. They could be the best in the city.

Iowa State Fair

Blue ribbons, butter cows (yes, a life-sized cow sculpted from butter), corn dogs and ice cream, husband-calling contests, cinnamon roll competition, and pork in abundant variations, including the state's biggest boar—in 2003 it was a pig named Pepperoni weighing in at over a thousand pounds. You'll find all this and more (lots more!) at the Iowa State Fair.

This is the state fair that inspired two Broadway plays and three movies, and is one of the most beloved in the Midwest. During its 11-day August run in Des Moines, over a million people come to admire the farm animals, peruse countless jars of jam and jelly, stand in awe of humungous garden vegetables, vie for prizes in hundreds of contests and, of course, eat.

Fair Food

From sugary funnel cakes and Gizmo sandwiches (seasoned sloppy-Joe style ground beef, topped with a slab of melt-y mozzarella cheese) to ribbon fries, kettle corn, lemon shake-ups, and fried Twinkies, the Fair is the place to sample just about anything that will never find a place on your dinner table at home.

And if it's on a stick, so much the better. Consider that most ubiquitous of all fair food—the dough-dipped, deep-fried hot dog, aka the corn dog.

As any proud Iowan will tell you, it was Melvin P. Little who brought the dough-encased, pork-centered treat to the Iowa State Fair in 1954. In fact, his daughter Helen Little still operates corn dog stands throughout the fairgrounds today. Some boast "bigger," some "better," and some "plumper." The truth is, no matter which stand you stop at, Iowa State Fair corn dogs are a cut above any you'll taste at other carnivals in the nation. Why? Helen Little concludes part of it has to do with the batter; her father and Pillsbury worked together

You've got to have a pork chop on a stick when you're at the Iowa State Fair.

to come up with a great-tasting dough to wrap the doggies in. The other part of it, of course, she admits, probably has something to do with the Iowa pork in the hot dogs.

But corn dogs are only one delicious way that Iowa pork is promoted at the fair. With the state ranked as the nation's top pork producer (one out of three jobs are porcine related) it stands to reason you'll also find plenty of ways to sample the "other white meat" here: Try it barbecued, pulled, roasted, grilled, or breaded into a tenderloin.

The best in my humble opinion? It's got to be that basic Iowa chop grilled over the open pit at the little stand right behind the Iowa Pork Producers dining hall. Here, when they say "on a stick," it refers to the actual bone of the pork chop—

so one is cautioned to "be careful, it's really hot" when the meat is handed over all foiled up, with the steaming bone sticking out as a handle.

I don't know, maybe it's the primeval thrill of sinking one's teeth into meat hot off the fire, holding onto it Neanderthal-style, but there really is nothing quite like eating one of these particular smoky pork chops. They're sweet, juicy, and tender. Still, if you prefer a more civilized dining situation, head into that Pork Producers hall. There's always a line (but they've got the system down and it moves fast). The Iowa chop here is memorable as well: supple, thick (over an inch!), and so tender you can easily cut it with the plastic knife provided. It's not quite so smoky. But you can eat it at a table . . . on a plate . . .

Ladies Welcome

Iowa state fairs are definitely family-oriented events. But in 1863, the secretary for the fair had to remind the men folk: "Do not be afraid to bring your wives and daughters. Parties having ladies in company will receive special consideration from the superintendent of the camp."

with a fork. And there's a bonus: the ice water here is free. Don't laugh. At the fair, on a blistering hot Iowa afternoon, ice water is a precious commodity.

Here's another pork tip. At a cute, brightly painted stand called The Wooden Shoe, you'll find specialties of Pella, Iowa—the Danish town of tulip fame. If you're there in the morning, get coffee for twenty-five cents and a Dutch Letter—flaky pastries shaped into alphabet letters and filled with rich almond paste. Lunch or dinner, order a piece of Pella bologna. This is ring bologna like Mom used to cook up, only they slice off a section of the seasoned sausage and put it on a stick. It's mildly Midwest spicy, and served sizzling hot. A bite into this and you'll never think of bologna as that thin, flat circle of blandness pressed between two slices of white bread anymore.

Perhaps though, the all-time favorite fair food can be found at Bauder's ice cream stand. Bauder's ice cream is made in the back room of a pharmacy in Des Moines, but in August you'll find it at the Fair as well. The first time I stopped at the stand, I couldn't resist a fresh peach shake; it was so thick with fresh peach bits and ice cream, there was no way I could suck it up with a straw

Sample a fresh peach shake or peppermint ice cream sandwich (handmade only at State Fair time) at the Bauder's Pharmacy booth.

(ask for a spoon). The second time I went back, I took my teenage son and his friend and we ordered their State Fair specialty, the peppermint ice cream sandwich, made only at Fair time. Loosely hand-wrapped in red and white checked tissue, the delectable treasure is a huge square of creamy smooth and rich vanilla ice cream flecked with chips of peppermint candy, sandwiched between thick chocolate cookies, and then frosted with rich dark fudge. Fair food doesn't get much better than this.

Food for Show

If you happen into the Blue Bunny-sponsored Maytag Family Center build-ing during the State Fair's Cinnamon Roll competition, be prepared. The over-whelming scent of cinnamon and spice is intoxicating. Banquet tables are laden with cinnamon rolls in every way, shape, and form. Some with nuts, some without. Frosted. Caramel. Basically, it looks like a magnificent morning feast in some happy dream.

With the winner receiving a whopping three thousand dollars in this com-petition, it's no wonder this is a well-entered contest. "It's the highest amount of prize money for a single state fair contest in the nation," says Arlette Hol-lister.

Besides overseeing the cinnamon roll contest, Hollister is the force behind all of the food judging that takes place during the Iowa State Fair. In 2003, she and 60-some helpers oversaw a grand total of 11,617 entries brought in by 883 contestants for contests that ranged from the cinnamon rolls to "cooking with lard" to "heirloom recipes made healthy." Premiums and prizes offered in 2003 were $58,117 in 180 divisions encompassing 894 classes.

One of the highlights of the Iowa State Fair: prize-winning pies on display.

These competitions are not just limited to, say, "pies," but specific pies: double crusted, cream, lattice-top cherry, black bottom, etc. Ditto for cakes: angel food, spice, layer, Bundt, whipped cream, devil's food, chiffon. Even kids get into the competition; the "Ugliest Cake" contest for youngsters is one of the most fun and popular.

Because of this large number of divisions and classes, judging begins even before the fair starts. After the fair actually commences, the judging goes on. You're welcome to watch as judges taste-test breads, cookies, pies, and more. When they're finished with each competition, one by one the judges tell the audience why they chose the particular cookie/bar/cake/fudge as a winner. It's a lesson in cookery as well as fun to watch.

But when you get tired of watching people eat in front of you, the Maytag Family Center also has cooking demonstrations on other stages here—and these usually involve some free samples plus helpful tips and handouts. Of course, don't forget to get your free Blue Bunny ice cream bar before you leave the center (the raspberry one is yum).

Some Prize-Winning Recipes

Cookies 'N' Cream Bars

Perennial champion Robin Tarbell-Thomas has won at least fifteen hundred blue ribbons at the Iowa State Fair during the 28 years she's been entering it. From her caramels, cookies, spaghetti sauce, jams, jellies, and more, she spends almost every night in June and July getting ready for the fair (that's not counting the preserving and canning she does all year long). In 2003, one of the blue ribbons she won was for Cookies 'N' Cream Bars in the Three-Layer Bars competition.

1/2 cup butter, softened

3/4 cup sugar

1 egg

1 teaspoon vanilla

1 cup all-purpose flour

3/4 cup graham cracker crumbs

1/3 cup cocoa

1 teaspoon baking powder

1/4 teaspoon salt

4 cookies 'n' cream flavored candy bars (1.55 ounces each)

11/2 cups marshmallow cream

Heat oven to 350 degrees. Grease an 8-inch-square baking pan. In large mixer bowl beat butter and sugar until light and fluffy. Add egg and vanilla; beat well. Stir together flour, graham cracker crumbs, cocoa, baking powder, salt; add to butter mixture, beating until blended.

Press half of the dough into prepared pan. Unwrap candy, break into pieces. Place candy and marshmallow cream in medium microwave-safe bowl. Microwave at high (100 percent) for 30 seconds; stir. If necessary, microwave at high for an additional 20 seconds at a time, stirring after each heating, until candy is melted and mixture is well-blended when stirred.

Spread candy mixture over dough in pan. Scatter bits of remaining dough over candy mixture. Carefully press to form layer. Bake 25 to 30 minutes or until dough is set and begins to pull from sides of pan. Cool completely in pan in wire rack. Cut into 16 bars. Drizzle chocolate bark (melted) on top of bars.

Chocolate Cream Cheese Cupcakes

The competition in the Chocolate Cupcakes category was limited to entrants ages 12 to 17, and netted Andrew Ward of Ankeny a blue ribbon in 2003. He's been entering recipes at the fair for several years.

Filling

1 8-ounce package cream cheese, softened

1 egg

$1/3$ cup granulated sugar

$1/3$ teaspoon salt

1 12-ounce package mini chocolate chips

Combine softened cream cheese, eggs, sugar and salt. Mix well. Blend in chocolate chips and set aside.

Cake

$1^1/2$ cups all purpose flour

1 cup granulated sugar

$1/4$ cup unsweetened cocoa

1 teaspoon baking soda

$1/2$ teaspoon salt

1 cup water

$1/2$ cup cooking oil

1 teaspoon vanilla

1 tablespoon vinegar

Sift together flour, sugar, cocoa, baking soda, and salt. Stir in water, oil, vanilla, and vinegar. Fill paper-lined cupcake pans $1/3$ full of batter. Top with $1^1/2$ teaspoon cheese mixture. Bake at 350 degrees for 15 to 20 minutes. Frost when cool.

Chocolate Frosting
2 cups powdered sugar

1 teaspoon vanilla

2 tablespoons butter

3 to 4 tablespoons milk

2 ounces melted unsweetened chocolate.

Mix all together until smooth, and then frost cupcakes.

Cajun Pork Burgers
Brett Toresdahl of West Des Moines won a ribbon for these hot and spicy burgers.

1 pound ground pork (you can use turkey too)

$3/4$ pound andouille sausage

1 rib celery

$1/2$ green bell pepper

5 green onions

2 teaspoons garlic powder

1 teaspoon thyme

1 tablespoon hot pepper sauce

salt and pepper

Remove casing from andouille sausage and grind sausage in a food processor. Finely chop vegetables and add to pork and sausage.
Add remaining ingredients and mix well to incorporate all. Form into six patties and cook in skillet about six to seven minutes per side. These burgers can also be prepared on the grill. Serve on buns with condiments of choice.
The recipes are courtesy of the winners and reprinted with permission.

Folks checking out the humongous garden vegetables at the fair.

W. E. Moranville's 10 Des Moines Food Favorites

W. E. Moranville has been the restaurant critic for the *Des Moines Register* since 1997. She grew up in Des Moines, Iowa, and has lived in New York City, England, and Ann Arbor. She also works as a cookbook editor and food writer.

Favorite Old Des Moines Italian Steakhouse: Gino's Restaurant and Lounge. This is your father's (or grandfather's) supper club; continuously operating since 1928, it will take you back to the days when Italian fried chicken or a plate of spaghetti and meatballs were a rare treat. While the bright, Christmas-red spaghetti sauce is distinctive, these days it's the steaks—quality aged cuts—that I head here for. 2809 Sixth Avenue, (515) 282-4029.

Favorite New Des Moines Italian Joint: Sam and Gabe's Italian Bistro. Run by a brother-and-sister team (who are, themselves, descendants of a beloved Des Moines restaurateur), this is the next generation of an Italian-American restaurant. They offer quite the sort of good-old Des Moines immigrant Italian dishes this town grew up on (e.g., lasagna, plus the best cannelloni on the planet), but they taste painstakingly made in small, fresh batches. The menu also nudges diners in new directions, with fresh seafood, good veal dishes, and more interesting ways with chicken than just about any other Italian restaurant. 8631 Hickman Road, Urbandale, (515) 271-9200.

Favorite Place for Steak de Burgo: Tursi's Latin King Restaurant. What? You don't know about Steak de Burgo? This is Des Moines' best-loved "you can only get it here" specialty. Many local steakhouses serve it, but this one's the best—a beautiful cut of beef tenderloin atop a bracing garlic-basil-butter sauce, with a firm, fresh mushroom cap on top. Though the Italian-American venue has been around since the 1930s, a Tuscan Villa makeover in the 90s gives the place an airy, open ambiance. Another menu highlight is the Chicken Spiedini. 2200 Hubbell Avenue, (515) 266-4466.

Favorite Bistro: Sage. If you're an inveterate foodie looking for the next head-turning bistro experience, head here. The inventive menu is tweaked with plenty of French and Italian influences, and they generally do great things with seafood. For a bold start to dinner, try the chicken-liver salad glazed with a warm bacon-studded balsamic vinaigrette. 6587 University Avenue, Windsor Heights, (515) 255-7722.

Favorite Wine Bar: Forty Three. A beautiful wine list, a knowledgeable staff, a menu of "small plates" (nibbles), and a gracious, warmly elegant setting (downtown in the historic Fort Des Moines Hotel) make this a lovely spot to unwind and discover some new-found favorite wines. 10th and Walnut, (515) 362-5224.

Favorite Bakery-Café: It's a two-way tie between two bakeries owned separately by two brothers. La Mie's offerings change often (and not just with the seasons!), so you never know quite what this lace is up to. Chances are that whatever they're doing will be fresh and creative—and the breads will be great. Basil Prosperi

East (in Des Moines's very up-and-coming East Village area) has a limited but committed artisanal cheese counter, terrific pastas and salads at lunch, and an intriguing price-fixed menu on weekend evenings. La Mie, 841 42nd Street, (515) 255-1625; Basil Prosperi, 407 East Fifth Street, (515) 243-9819.

Best Spot for an "I Can't Believe This Is Des Moines" Experience: There are two; they're owned by the same people and they're both downtown. The Royal Mile is a perfect (and perfectly cozy) English pub, with solid pub fare. The Hessen Haus is a German beer hall, complete with oompah music, mammoth steins of frothy-topped beer, rosy-cheeked clients, and hearty beer-hall food. Royal Mile, 210 Fourth Street, (515) 280-3771; Hessen Haus 101 Fourth Street, (515) 288-2520.

Favorite Spot for a Special Lunch: Des Moines Art Center Restaurant. If you're from out of town, you absolutely, positively must visit the Des Moines Art Center, a world-class gem of a museum. While here, take in one of the inspired lunches of fresh, seasonal, creative cuisine, served (in temperate months) on a lovely courtyard terrace or (otherwise) in the pleasant dining room. 4700 Grand Ave, (515) 271-0332.

Favorite Thai Restaurant: Thai Flavors. The simple (but at least they try) atmosphere is not the draw, though if you're hankering for great Thai food, this is your spot. Even people in from such Asian-cuisine hot spots as Seattle and New York are surprised at the amazing intrigues of flavor found here. Try the Green Curry and Tom Ka Kai (a coconut-laced chicken soup). 1254 East 14th Street, (515) 262-4658.

Favorite Downtown Hot Spot: Centro. If you want to be where it's at, head to this happening urban eatery. With soaring ceilings, banquette seating, and a swish crowd, it's as "big city" as Des Moines gets. Try the wood-grilled specialties. If you're on a budget, you can still have all that irresistible "where it's at" bustle for the price of a pizza. 1011 Locust Street, (515) 244-7033.

Northeast Region

Pies, Picnics, and Norwegian Pancakes

Fresh-from-the-oven pies and picnics by small sparkling waterfalls are just two of the pleasures afforded visitors who venture to the northeast section of Iowa. In the most easterly part of the region, you'll find steep bluffs and wooded hills, scenic vistas and small, tidy towns where church bells chime on the hour and Saturday morning farmers' markets are set up on the corner of the main street.

One of the largest communities in this land of bluffs and valleys is Decorah. Home to Luther College, the town is surrounded by pretty parks, hiking and biking trails, even caves. It's also home to the Vesterheim Norwegian–American Museum, the nation's largest and oldest museum dedicated to telling the story of immigrants from one nation. This is a town proud of its Norwegian heritage, and you'll find signs of it everywhere. From the gnome figurines in private flower gardens to cafés in town serving up Norwegian specialties like *lefse, rommegrot* (a thickened and rich cream pudding), and Norwegian pancakes.

There are many beautiful spots for a picnic around Decorah, but one in particular I love is the small Dunning's Spring Park, with its lovely waterfall and picturesque wedge of greenery. Don't be surprised to see people setting up for an occasional wedding out here either.

From Decorah, a few miles takes you to Spillville. Settled by Czech immigrants, Spillville is home to the Bily Clocks Museum, and also quite proud of a former resident, the famed Czech composer Antonin Dvorak, who spent a summer here in the late 1800s. If you have time, you should stop at the Old World Inn. Famous for its *kolaches*, it serves meals that feature many Czech recipes.

A popular drive for Luther College students on a Saturday afternoon is Gunder, and The Shanti restaurant. The reason? It cooks up something called a Gunderburger—a full pound of specially seasoned ground beef shaped into a big dinner plate-sized burger and served with all sorts of toppings.

South of Gunder, you'll drive into one of the prettiest towns in the state: Elkader. Tucked into the bluffs along the banks of the Turkey River, it's a town that has it all—the bustling been-there-forever corner bakery and a deli and meat market next door, where warm pies make their appearance about 11 a.m. for the "pie table." There's the pharmacy . . . the hardware store. Saturday mornings, in front of the historic and beautiful 1888 Keystone Bridge, a local farmer or two may set up tables with fresh produce: asparagus in the spring, corn in the summer. Church bells ring out across the river on the hour. What more could you want?

Almost smack-dab in the center of northern Iowa, near the Minnesota border, there's Clear Lake. Probably best known for its Surf Ballroom—the site of Buddy Holly's last concert, February 3, 1959. Holly, along with Ritchie Valens and J. P. "The Big Bopper" Richardson, died in a plane crash north of Clear Lake following the evening's performance. It's not exactly easy finding the crash site (there's a small memorial there), with directions given as "past the grain bins . . . to the first fence row on the left" . . . but it can be found. And believe it or not, when you walk out here—single file on a dirt path next to the corn stalks—you may even meet a couple more people out paying their respects. The little shrine includes all sorts of quirky items left by fans: bouquets of sun-faded fake flowers, beads, coins, and even business cards.

Back in Clear Lake, do check out the ballroom, little changed from 1959. Original wooden booths are decorated with fish and bubbles, there's a cloud-studded ceiling and South Sea murals, all restored to their 1948 appearance. Ladies: do take a look-see in the cavernous women's bathroom. You can easily imagine a long-ago dance night, with clusters of giggling girls in here, applying red lipstick in front of the mirror, adjusting slips and bobby socks.

Clear Lake hosts the Lakeside DixieFest in July, a fun time to visit; it's part of a full weekend of arts-related events during Lakefest. Bands alternate one-hour concerts on the stage in the park, and an Art "Sail" is set up on the grounds as well—an annual event with 85 artists selling and displaying their works. You can also walk to the waterfront where the Lady of the Lake (a double-decker excursion boat) is docked. Take a sunset cruise, or simply put down a blanket by the beach and watch the sailboats race across the water.

For another nudge of nostalgia, get off I-35 near Williams and take a half hour to drive to Iowa Falls. Here, the Princess Café is a gorgeous, almost-untouched example of art deco style. The added bonus at the Princess is that you can also get a gooey, rich chocolate and caramel sundae, served in a vintage tulip-shaped ice cream glass, at the soda fountain. (Just get there before 2 p.m.—the place closes at that time until it re-opens for dinner.)

On your way back to the freeway, you can go through the Boondocks. The real Boondocks. Who knew the Boondocks were in Iowa? It's actually a truck stop, and it serves up fantastic biscuits and cinnamon rolls.

Decorah

Whippy Dip
130 College Drive, Phone: (563) 382-4591

Nobody who has attended college in Decorah forgets the Whippy Dip. It's just one of those beloved Decorah traditions. Like the girls wearing "I'm a Quality Chick" T-shirts from the Quality Chick Hatchery in town.

Right next to the Decorah Bicycles, you can't miss the building. A row of Scandinavian flags flies outside and the street-side picnic tables are usually filled with people. Day and night, even at 10 in the morning when it opens, there are people lining up for a scoop of the sweet soft-serve stuff.

Current owners Rosie and Greg Carolan say they haven't been running the shop that long— "only 17 years"—because after all, the previous owners had started it in 1952. Rosie remembers working at the stand before she and Greg owned it. Greg recalls delivering bread and ice cream mix before they decided to buy the place.

Since then, they've been keeping the kids (and adults) in town happy making the usual repertoire of ice cream favorites—malts, shakes, sundaes (try the hot apple topping), cones, something called Slushy Whips (they're ice cream mixed with ice), and Tornados. Basically, a Tornado is the ice cream of your choosing, and then you "beat the heck out of it" with the candy of your choice: Peanut M&M'S, Butterfinger, Kit Kat, even gummi bears. After that, one more big, soft scoop of ice cream goes on top. Everybody has their favorites, and while the candy bars are contenders for most popular mix-ins, the chocolate chip cookie dough could be the top Tornado of choice. When school is in session, Rosie says she makes up to 60 pounds of the chocolate chip cookie dough (there are no raw eggs in this mixture) daily.

Sure, the tornado sounds suspiciously similar to something offered at other ice cream franchises around. But see, it's not that you can't get ice cream like this anywhere else. The point is that this is the Whippy Dip—and nobody leaves Decorah without a stop at the Whippy Dip. It's just what you do.

Nobody leaves Decorah without a stop at the Whippy Dip.

Mabe's Pizza
110 East Water Street, Phone: (563) 382-4297

Mabe's is a local favorite that serves a full menu, complete with pastas, broasted chicken, hamburgers, and even seafood, but you can't beat its pizza and a pitcher of 1919 Root Beer. Families and students from Luther College in town fill the booths and tables, and the pizza has such a reputation with the college crowd that Mabe's freezes the pies and takes them to alumni events all over the country.

Nothing fancy or out of the ordinary in the décor at this always-busy spot, but do notice the rosemaling (a form of decorative flower painting that developed in Norway) on the one wall. The different-sized rosemaled "plates" are not really for decoration though; these are for showing the actual sizes of pizzas available for ordering—rather appropriate in this town with its strong Norwegian heritage.

Pizza here comes on a very thin, crispy crust (thick crust available on request), and you can load it with the standard stuff: pepperoni, sausage, green peppers, and so forth, or go for something a step more adventurous—maybe the taco pizza pie. No matter what you order, it's plenty filling, it's fairly cheap, and the service is always super nice.

Nordic Fest

Held on the last full weekend of July, this annual event has been going on in Decorah since 1966, celebrating the community's Norwegian heritage with music, entertainment, and, of course, food. You can expect to find a variety of Scandinavian delicacies, including *lefse*, *rommegrot*, *smorbrod*, and others, in addition to those melt-on-the-tongue wonderful pastries like kringle, *krumkakke*, and *sandbakkels*.

Gunder

The Shanti
17455 Gunder Road, Phone: (563) 864-9289

This little wooden structure located in tiny Gunder (population, maybe 32) sits across from a small, old church and its surrounding cemetery on a peaceful country corner intersection. Owned by Brenda and Jeff Pfister since 1992, the community gathering spot is well-known by college students in nearby

Decorah as well as locals far and wide for something called a Gunderburger. "That's the biggest hamburger you'll ever see," I was told in Elkader at the full-service gas station. "Oh, and don't forget to order the hash browns too."

The building is part bar, part hometown café—and you can order all sizes of burgers and brews. But most folks come here for the full pound of seasoned ground beef that's shaped to the size of a dinner plate (a large dinner plate!), cooked to juicy perfection, and topped with a bun that's more for decoration. This is the famous Gunderburger. And it's definitely for sharing. Unless, of course, you're a football player in training. Or a very hungry college student who has driven down from Decorah.

Postville

Jacob's Table (in Jacob's Market)
121 West Greene
Street, Phone:
(563) 864-7087

Home to a large kosher packing plant, the unassuming small town of Postville also happens to have one of the best kosher markets and restaurants you'll find anywhere in the Midwest: Jacob's Table. Don't be surprised to hear Hebrew and English with Brooklyn accents while you're shopping here either. (The store has even been featured on Food Network). Shelves are lined with things like packages of Osem chicken noodle soup mix, and the genie-like bottles of Sabra Orange Chocolate Liqueur. A takeout counter offers lox, smoked herring, and hummus, and kosher lunches and dinners are served here too. If you call and order *challah* on Thursday, you can pick it up on Friday.

In Postville, Jacob's Table is one of the Midwest's best kosher markets and restaurants.

Elkader

Elkader Deli and Meat Market
105 North Main Street, Phone: (563) 245-3313

Next door to Pedretti's Bakery, the deli and meat market offers up perfect picnic fixings to go with the bread you just bought at the bakery. There are cheeses, and meats from Edgewood Locker—pastrami, honey ham, smoked turkey. You can also pick up smoked chops, seasonal brats, and an incredibly marvelous "cottage bacon"—which resembles Canadian bacon. Fried up, it smells as divine as it tastes. It's a great alternative to standard bacon in a BLT because, for one thing, it's sliced in a round.

If you are at the deli around 11:00 a.m. on a Tuesday through Saturday, though, you're in for the best treat and show in town. This is when the home-baked pies start coming out of the oven, and are delivered to the "pie table" in the front of the store. Usually there are six tempting pies (all baked in different pie plates): maybe pumpkin, pecan, apple, strawberry, peach, and coconut cream. These are carefully carried out and lovingly displayed on a long table by the front door, under signs that say, appropriately, "DIET? What DIET?" Folks come in and help themselves to a slice of pie, then grab a cup of coffee and sit down at one of the many tables in the room for afternoon coffee break.

These pies are some of the best you're going to find anywhere—with dazzling, flaky, thin crusts made by someone who obviously has been making pies (and a lot of them) for many, many years.

The "pie table" at the Elkader Deli and Meat Market.

Pedretti's Bakery
101 North Main, Phone: (563) 245-1280

Crossing the stone arch bridge into Elkader, you'll easily see the turquoise corner storefront with its sign "Pedretti's" hanging out front indicating the bakery. Open the old-fashioned heavy screen door, and inside you'll find a cozy, warm, scented space that's always busy with customers—not to mention punctuated by the occasional loud and bold ringing of a real telephone. (Pedretti's black classic telephone—yes, the kind you actually need your pointer finger to twirl the spin dial—sits on a tabletop near the cash register.)

Behind the counter, shelves are loaded with breads, including seven grain, caraway rye, Vienna, and raisin. Below, glass display shelves entice with angel food cakes, doughnuts, cream horns, turnovers, frosted cupcakes, bismarcks, and brownies. Cookies fill another case: chewy and spicy gingerbread men, plus raspberry filled cookies, icebox, macadamia nut, and a dessert-plate-sized chocolate sandwich cookie (two chocolate rounds slathered with frosting in between) that's sinfully sweet and not to be missed. Retro prices too: breads from $1.15 for a basic home-baked loaf up to a whopping $2.60 for a loaded-with-raisin loaf.

Clear Lake

Cabin Coffee Company
303 Main Avenue, Phone: (641) 357-6500

With real saddles to sit in, and coffee blends like the earthy and intense Cowboy, sweet and bold Saddle Creek, or the full-bodied Wrangler, this is one independent coffeehouse you're not likely to forget.

I've been zipping off the freeway here (it's about the halfway point from Minneapolis to Des Moines) for coffee beans, iced espressos, and double skim lattes ever since I discovered the place. In my advocacy for folks to get off the freeway and take five extra minutes to drive into the bypassed town, this place is one of the treasures you can find.

There's comfy log furniture, a large rock fireplace. You can pick up your e-mail, even have a bowl of Kickin' Crab Sweet Corn Chowder or a fresh-baked scone. The owners roast coffee beans daily, or you can pick your own green beans, specify how you want them roasted, and they'll do it for you while you wait.

The place is also near a couple very nice antique stores, I might add, and that's the other great thing about getting off the freeway and stopping in town. You can do a little shopping. Of course, I suppose that means the last cup of coffee I had here cost me $150—but hey, that little vintage glass-doored bookcase was still a steal.

The Best Coffeehouses in Iowa

In 2003, Chuck Offenburger, long-time Iowa writer, invited readers of his Web site, www.offenburger.com, to nominate their favorite Iowa coffeehouses. From that list, he and Mark Redenbaugh, owner of Abner Bell's Coffeehouse in Storm Lake, traveled the state, reviewing about 30 of the java joints that were nominated. From those, Offenburger came up with the following list, along with his notes.

Points were awarded for coffeehouses that did their own roasting and have regular live entertainment and other scheduled programs. Points were also given to coffeehouses that seemed to act as community gathering places, especially if the places attracted people of all ages. Points were taken away if coffeehouses allowed cigarette, cigar, and pipe smoking. Offenburger also felt it unfair to consider coffeehouses open for less than a year in the top 10, so the best of those went under the category "Rookies of the Year." Obviously, even more coffeehouses have opened since this survey, so keep a lookout.

The Top 10

1. Java Joe's Coffeehouse, Des Moines

2. The Java House, 211 1/2 East Washington Street, downtown Iowa City

3. Zanzibar's Coffee Adventure, Des Moines

4. Stomping Grounds, Ames

5. Abner Bell's Coffeehouse, Storm Lake

6. Saints Rest Coffee House, Grinnell

7. Smokey Row Coffee House and Soda Fountain, Pella

8. Linden St. Coffee House, Lamoni

9. Cup of Joe, Cedar Falls

10. Pierce Street Coffee Works, Sioux City

Honorable Mention (and highly recommended)

Revelations, Fairfield

Jitters, Sioux City

Friedrichs Coffee, 86th Street, Urbandale

The Sanctuary, Shenandoah

Brewed Awakenings, Cedar Rapids

Santa Fe Espresso, Ames

Magpie Coffeehouse, Decorah

Boulevard Joe's, Dubuque

The Daily Grind, Algona

Theo's Java Hut, Davenport

Jay's Java Garden, Adel

Bloomers on Central Gourmet Coffee and Gift Shoppe, Fort Dodge

Once Upon a Thyme Coffee, Public Library, Fort Dodge

Rookies of the Year (recently opened)

Higher Grounds Coffee House & Emporium, Mount Pleasant

Café Manna Java, Dubuque

Miguel's Coffee Bar, Dubuque

The Bread Basket, Historic Fourth Street, Sioux City

Cabin Coffee Company, Clear Lake

Nhu Y Café Shop, Sioux City

The Copper Cup, Cherokee

Bookends & Beans, Decorah

Starbucks, downtown Des Moines

Grinnell Coffee Company, Grinnell

Best On-Campus College Coffeehouse

Marty's CyberCafé, Centennial Union, Luther College, Decorah

Honorable Mention: Holy Grounds at Smith Chapel, Simpson College, Indianola; The Konditorie at Vogel Library, Wartburg College, Waverly; and Stomping Grounds, Gage Memorial Union, Coe College, Cedar Rapids.

Unexpected Bonus: Best Piece of Pie I've Had in 55 Years of Pie Eating

Lemon coconut, made by Mary Peterson at The Sanctuary, Shenandoah

Reprinted with permission from www.offenburger.com

Docks
475 North Shore Drive, Phone: (641) 357-6338

A grand old lakeside eatery with sand-in-your-shoes appeal, Docks probably has more guests arriving by boat than by car.

Décor consists of at-the-lake memorabilia, but truthfully, the room doesn't need much of anything—the wall of windows overlooking the sparkling lake is the best view in town. You can watch the action on the water and, if you time it right, even catch a sunset.

The menu is varied: Burgers and grilled chicken sandwiches are offered along with supper club fare like pan-seared filet mignon and sauteed lemon and garlic shrimp (seafood is flown in daily from Maine). More elegant entrees include crab-filled French turbot with white wine sauce and New Zealand rack of lamb with red wine sauce. One of the most delicious items on the menu is probably one of the most unlikely for a lakeside eatery in Iowa: Swedish meatballs with lingonberries and mashed potatoes.

Desserts are good too: try the white chocolate raspberry cheesecake or mocha cappuccino torte with bing cherries.

More folks arrive by boats than cars at the Docks restaurant in Clear Lake.

FAQs at Docks

Here are a few of the most frequently asked questions at Docks in Clear Lake (according to the back of the menu).

Do you take wet money? Sure.

Does the lake freeze in winter? Yep.

What do you do in the winter? The same as we do in the summer, but a whole lot less.

When's our food coming? As quickly as possible. We're not a fast-food establishment. If you're in a hurry, please come back when you have time to enjoy fabulous food in a friendly lakeside atmosphere.

Courtesy of Docks and reprinted with permission.

McKenna's Blues, Booze and BBQ
444 North Shore Drive, Phone: (641) 357-1443

This little barbeque joint next to the famous Surf Ballroom is a seasonal outpost of McKenna's Barbeque in Omaha. But instead of a lot of blues memorabilia around, it has old Buddy Holly posters on the walls.

No matter, the barbeque here is topnotch. There are only about 10 tables (and they fill up fast), but there's always takeout. (McKenna's does a brisk carryout business.)

There's plenty to choose from, and you can never go wrong with the baby back ribs. But to get a taste of it all, the thing to order here is the Three Way, which nets you a big platter full of smoked St. Louis-style ribs, smoked chicken, and McKenna's smoked brisket. In typical barbeque house fashion, you also get some sides with your meat. Here the excellent jalapeno cornbread comes with honey butter, there's spicy baked beans, and corn on the cob. The lush-with-flavor sauce comes on the side in a little paper cup.

When you're done here, it's just a few steps to the Surf—where rock-'n'-roll memories reign supreme.

Barrel Drive-In
206 US Highway 18 W, Phone: (641) 357-2600

This old drive-in with the huge chicken out front is a classic in Clear Lake—one of those venerable summertime institutions that families return to year after year. What is it about sitting in the car and sipping a root beer float, eating broasted chicken (the Barrell's is top of the charts—crispy and not greasy), and chowing down onion rings (these are good here too) that is just so appealing on a summer night? Carhop service is friendly, and the whole experience totally retro and fun.

A Picnic by the Lake

There are several places in Clear Lake for takeout, but two favorite choices are the Starboard Market or Ge-Jo's By-the-Lake. Ge-Jo's buttery, puffy, crispy pizza (order the white-sauced one with anchovy) is awesome.

Mason City

Marjorie's Tea House and Gift Shop
320 South Pennsylvania, Phone: (641) 421-8066

When you've finished touring the Music Man Square in town, head over to Marjorie's Tea House and its brief, but imaginative and delightful, lunch menu. The tall, old-fashioned house with the pretty pink flowering bush out front is conveniently located next door to Meredith Willson's boyhood home (you can tour his house after lunch). An unfussy room, the tables are set with linens, goblets, and teapots for centerpieces. Old photos hang on the walls. Some even reveal the original owner of the house (Marjorie) as a little girl, standing on the porch with a group of young neighborhood children, among them the later-to-be-famous Meredith, who was the born the same year as she was.

Menu selections are seasonal and change monthly, but combine tried-and-true favorites like Marjorie's chicken salad sandwich, fresh with oranges, grapes, and almonds for example, along with offerings like vegetarian lasagna (from a Croatian recipe) that incorporates feta cheese in the dish. Complimentary rosemary bread arrives warm in a basket. (You can smell the bread baking from the street.) The rosemary bread was first made at Marjorie's for a party they hosted for Meredith Willson's widow Rosemary (she lives out of state now, but still visits occasionally.) The bread caught on, and has since become a signature of the tearoom's lunches.

Desserts here are yummy, and if proprietor Steve Musson's dense chocolatey brownie with ice cream and made-from-scratch butterscotch sauce is one of the choices, do order it.

Pro's Sandwich Shop
629 South Federal Avenue, Phone: (641) 424-2662

Drive by this place at lunch and you could miss it, unless you happen to catch a glimpse of the parking lot beside it. Then you can't help but notice the cars pulling into the parking lot and the steady stream of people going in and out.

This is the kind of place where bowling trophies are proudly displayed by the cash register and the counter stretches out and around the big room, although there are a few tables squeezed against the walls. It's definitely a local spot.

Diner food is what to order here, so keep it simple. Order a root beer (it comes in a frosty mug) or a milk shake and an egg salad sandwich, grilled cheese, or a Beef Delight (another name for the Iowa loosemeat or Tavern). This version of the loosemeat sandwich comes wrapped in a green and white checked paper, and it's another winner.

Cedar Falls

Cedar Falls Wine and Tulips Festival

May in the Midwest. Buds are bursting, snow has melted (usually), and it's time once again for tulips and wine.

Since 1985, "An Evening in Celebration of Wine and Tulips" has been taking place at the University of Northern Iowa in Cedar Falls. Attending this event is a great way to sample a whole lot of wines (over two hundred, including some regional wines), taste some Midwestern cheeses and bread, listen to live music, support public radio stations KUNI and KHKE, and best all, celebrate that winter's over and summer's on its way.

Maucker Union at the university is decorated with bunches of colorful tulips, and your ticket gets you admission, an etched souvenir wine glass, and a helpful detailed wine guide booklet.

During the evening, a silent auction also takes place. If you're a fan of internationally acclaimed Cedar Falls artist Gary Kelley's annual gorgeous posters for the event (I am), you can call (800) 772-2440 or (319) 273-6400, ext. 0, on weekdays to purchase a signed poster from any of the past years. You can order your advance tickets for the event at the same time.

Iowa Wineries

Long considered the Corn State, Iowa boasts a growing wine industry that has seen acreage under vine increasing rapidly in

111

recent years. With soils that vary greatly (from those high in clay to those that are gravel-based), the regions that are showing the greatest potential for vineyards are in the westward Loess Hills area and in the northeast, with its limestone-based soils and steep slopes that stretch over some 20 miles.

Ackerman Winery and Gifts, Amana. This winery has the distinct honor of being the oldest winery operated by one family in the state of Iowa. Located in the historic Amana Colonies, Ackerman Winery brings three generations of experience to producing quality, award-winning fruit, dinner, and dessert wines.

Eagle City Winery, Iowa Falls. Founded in 1991 by Dr. Ken Groninga and his wife Carolyn, this winery offers a scenic view into the workings of a small vineyard that produces 12 wine varieties including merlot, cabernet sauvignon, chardonnay, Riesling, rhubarb, and a dessert wine.

Ehrle Brothers Winery, Homestead. With knowledge acquired in Germany more than a century ago, Ehrle Brothers was founded in 1934. Today, it is Iowa's oldest operating winery and is home to the original Lover's Wine, made with the Amana Church recipe.

The Grape Vine Winery, Main Amana. Here, wine lovers can sample 16 varieties of wines made from family recipes that are generations old.

Heritage Winery and Cheese Haus, Amana. The Heritage winery offers 22 varieties of unusual wines, including cranberry, apricot, plum, peach, honey, and black currant. Visitors to the winery can also partake of more than 40 kinds of domestic and imported cheeses available for daily sampling.

La Vida Loca Winery, Indianola. The Putz family produces fine country fruit wines including blackberry, cherry, elderberry, raspberry, wild grape, and gooseberry.

Little Amana Winery, Amana. Since 1971, Little Amana Winery has made delicious fruit and fine table wines. The winery also features a gift shop with glassware and crystal as well as unique bar and beverage items.

Old Wine Cellar Winery, Amana. Established in 1961, Old Wine Cellar uses century-old wine making methods to produce its award-winning varieties. Old Wine Cellar wines are also available in select stores and area restaurants.

Sandstone Winery, Amana. Opened in 1960 in a century-old home made of native sandstone, the Sandstone Winery offers wines made from whole fruits. The entire wine process—crushing, pressing, fermenting, bottling, and labeling—is completed on the premises.

Summerset Winery, Indianola. Ron Mark began planting grapes in 1989. Today the vineyard has grown to 12 acres and produces 86,000 bottles of wine annually. Visitors to the winery can also stay at the bed and breakfast on the property, but reservations are necessary.

Tabor Home Vineyards and Winery, Amana. Named for the family's original 1870s farm, the uniquely designed winery has a large, airy tasting room overlooking the vineyard and wine production facility. Tabor Home offers 19 wine varieties. One thousand five hundred of the 9,000 gallons of wine produced here come from their own vineyards.

Village Winery, Amana. Don and Eunice Krauss founded the Village Winery in 1973, offering two varieties of wine, grape and rhubarb. Today, the winery offers 15 varieties of wine, produced and bottled on the premises from formulas handed down to Don by his father and grandfather.

There are many other wineries in Iowa, including Christian Herschler District Winery, Donnellson; Eagles Landing Winery, Marquette; Little Swan Lake Winery, Estherville; and Village Vintner, Amana.

A Food-Friendly Place to Stay

The Blackhawk Hotel
115 Main Street
Phone: (319) 277-1161; (800) 488-4295

Listed on the National Register of Historic Places, the Blackhawk in Cedar Falls is the oldest continuously operating hotel site in Iowa. A glimpse into the stunning lobby gives only a hint at what they've done to renovate this place. Even if you're not staying here, ask for a tour of the guest rooms if possible. The upstairs rooms and suites are impressive, accented with antiques and windows that look over the charming historic Main Street, with its old-fashioned street lamps, unique shops, and eateries. Marble bathrooms, Jacuzzi tubs, luxurious linens—all are part of the modern conveniences offered. But the fun of staying here is also partly due to the history in the halls and the character of the building. The other nice thing about staying at the Blackhawk is simply its location—on historic Main Street in downtown Cedar Falls. Because for the most part, once you park the car, you won't need it again.

In the lobby, late afternoons (or after a grueling road trip) you can stop in The Stuffed Olive for a fresh martini. Or you can walk up a block to a great little wine and chocolate shop called Indulgences; buy a truffle or get a glass of wine and relax out back on their patio. You can even purchase a bottle of wine to take back to the hotel, if you're so inclined (and you should, especially if you're staying in one of the suites with a spacious sitting area).

In the morning, it's just a few steps to the Cup of Joe coffeehouse for your espresso. This place is straight out of the 1950s with its Formica-topped kitchen table and chair sets.

After lunch, you can use one of the bicycles available at the hotel and go for a ride on the Cedar Valley Bike Trail (it's also close to the hotel). For dinner, check out the nearby Montage restaurant. They do some incredibly fine things, like a blackberry pork tenderloin served over lemon couscous. *Wine Spectator* has given them the Award of Excellence designation for their selections for two years in a row.

After dessert and coffee, it's simply a short stroll back to the hotel.

Iowa Falls

Princess Grill and Pizzeria
607 Washington Avenue, Phone: (641) 648-9602

A seat in one of the beautiful African mahogany booths at the back of the Princess Café is a time machine. Of course, so is a seat at the 25-foot-long soda fountain in the front here, complete with the original stools and fountain equipment. (It's thought to be the largest remaining marble soda fountain in the U.S.)

The town sweet shop since 1935, the Princess is an outstanding example of the art deco style. The cool façade features black Carrara glass with a pale green design at the corners and sides. In 1935, the neon sign out front was one of the largest in central Iowa. Inside, the hard terrazzo floors were poured by hand and then ground to a smooth finish. The red, white, and blue neon lights symbolized how much love these men had for their new country.

The building (which replaced a brick building that burned on Christmas Day 1934) also was the first building in town to be air-conditioned. The original cardboard sign that advertised such an amazing perk in here—a rarity for a building in the 1930s—is even on display in one of the old glass candy display cases in the front of the store.

The Princess today is much more than an ice cream and sweet shop, though; it's a full service restaurant, serving lunches and dinners. But the main attractions, especially come summer time, are its swoonfully indulgent soda fountain specialties. Malts and sundaes, sodas and phosphates, and banana splits in four different variations. Besides the traditional, at the Princess you can get a fruit split, strawberry split, or a hot fudge split.

Specialty sundaes feature a Golden Cashew (butter pecan ice cream drenched in caramel topping, piled with cashews) or an Almond Joy (vanilla ice cream smothered in hot fudge, sprinkled with coconut and a spoonful of almonds).

Although candy is no longer being made here, the marble slab that was used for its production is still in the basement. (It's too big and too heavy to move, according to Minette Zaimes, who owns the café with her husband Tom.) On the main floor, the antique candy display cases now showcase more of the shop's history. The whole place is a great peek into the past.

They really don't make places like this any more. Make sure to visit.

The Boondocks USA

Actually, the Boondocks is not really a town. It's a truck stop at Exit 144 off Interstate 35, and the place is a must-stop if your sense of humor runs to the offbeat and you're hankering for a hamburger.

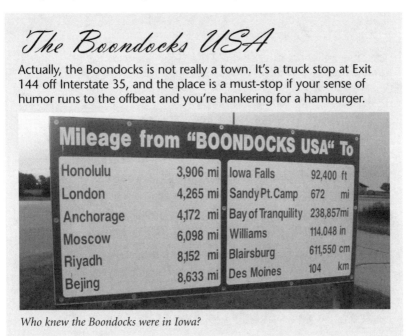

Mileage from "BOONDOCKS USA" To			
Honolulu	3,906 mi	Iowa Falls	92,400 ft
London	4,265 mi	Sandy Pt. Camp	672 mi
Anchorage	4,172 mi	Bay of Tranquility	238,857mi
Moscow	6,098 mi	Williams	114.048 in
Riyadh	8,152 mi	Blairsburg	611,550 cm
Bejing	8,633 mi	Des Moines	104 km

Who knew the Boondocks were in Iowa?

Beyond the parking lot, for example, not far from the picnic area, there's a fire hydrant with a sign that reads "City Dogs." Next to it, there's a tree stump with a sign for "Country Dogs." Across the truck lot, in a grassy area, there's an old Volkswagen bug with flowers growing out of its roof.

The café is the typical trucker's sort—a counter in the front, booths and tables further back. But the food is awesome. In the morning, do not miss the warm-from-the-oven biscuits. Slathered with a little butter and jam, they can't be beat. Cinnamon rolls are huge, the pies homemade. Hamburgers are juicy and hand-pattied.

Outside, there's a sign displaying the distances from the Boondocks to various places in the world (and, in keeping with the true spirit of the place, given in a variety of measurements). There's Honolulu (3,906 miles), Beijing (8,633 miles), the Bay of Tranquility (238,857 miles—it's on the moon), Des Moines (104 kilometers), Blairsburg (611,550 centimeters), Iowa Falls (92,400 feet), Williams (114.048 inches).

You'll want to stop and get a photo—proof that you really were in the Boondocks.

Jim Duncan's 10 Iowa Food Favorites

Jim Duncan writes the column "The Good Steward," is the editorial director of *Relish*, an Iowa food quarterly, the food writer for the weekly *Pointblank-Des Moines*, and author of the "Taste of Iowa" features in *The Iowan* magazine.

My list would change every time someone asked me.

Seed Saver's Orchard, Decorah. Pick your own apples in autumn.

Ivy Bake Shoppe and Café, Fort Madison. Butter and cream baked goods.

Polehna's Meat Market, Cedar Rapids. Meatloaf, sold out by 10 a.m. every Friday and Saturday.

La Rosa, Des Moines. Freshly made, fresh masa tamales, Michoac·an style, in corn husks, not banana leaves.

Broom Factory, Cedar Falls. Emu burgers.

Tastee In and Out Drive-In, Sioux City. Onion chips,

nowhere else in America, the inspiration of the new Broadway play Onion Girl, too. Plus, the Sioux City specialty, the Tavern sandwich.

Archie's Waeside, Le Mars. Bob Rand's aged steaks are great, the family garden supplies the veggies, but the best-in-state burgers are my choice here.

Four Seasons Café, Des Moines. Breakfast at 5 a.m. Farm-fresh eggs, hash browns from scratch, cast of characters. Small town café in the city.

Bistro Montage and 25th Street Café, Des Moines. Enosh Kelley's treatment of Milt Sheeder's chicken and Larry Cleverley's fresh greens.

Second Street Coffee House, Fairfield. Coffee drinks made with Radiance organic milk from grass-fed cows, milk as it used to taste.

East Central Region

Kolaches and Dandelion Wine

East Central Iowa is a study in contrasts. On the one hand, you've got the old-world charm of the Amana Colonies—properly neat villages connected with country roads, fireflies flickering at night, family-style meals. On the other hand, there's the cosmopolitan vibe that a high-energy college town like Iowa City presents: Indian restaurants, coffeehouses with jazz playing at night, and bookstores filled with literary treasures.

Around the Amish country of Kalona, horse-drawn buggies share the highways and it's not uncommon to see women in long black dresses and bonnets. But stop in Mount Vernon (and the Lincoln Café) and you'd swear this charmingly hip college town was set down here from out east somewhere.

Drive into the Czech Village in Cedar Rapids and you're back in the old world again—complete with a bakery serving up *kolaches* and a family meat market still making up its Czech specialties according to generations old recipes.

The region is filled with this juxtaposition of old and new—the past mingling with the future, constantly pushing us on ahead, but keeping us grounded even as we speed on through.

The historic centerpiece of the region is the Amana Colonies, with tidy brick villages, homegrown wines, quiet country roads, well-kept gardens. Not much

Amana hams are famous for good reason.

has changed here since the 1850s when the Amana Colonies were founded by a group of German religious dissenters. Originally owned and operated collectively, in 1932 the commune (contrary to many folks' belief, the Amana Colonies are not Amish) broke up into a church and for-profit corporation.

Today, many businesses are still independently owned and operated—including several restaurants serving up the legendary Amana Colonies German fare. In fact, it's long been known that the family-style food served here is one of the main reasons folks visit the Amana Colonies—and continue making it the number-one tourist attraction in the state.

Historically, the Amana Colonies' reputation for good eats commenced during its communal era when there were more than 50 kitchen houses serving five meals daily to the colonists; and even at that time visitors were known to come here to enjoy the delicious offerings.

Nowadays, mealtime finds visitors at several tables throughout the colonies. In Homestead, Zuber's Family Style Restaurant serves traditional German food like *wienerschnitzel* with *spaetzle* as well as slow-baked country-style chicken and thick slices of that wonderful smoked Amana ham—all within a cozy room complete with lace curtains on the windows and shiny polished wood floor. Surprisingly, baseball memorabilia can also be found on the walls; this relates to the major-league career of its founder.

Baseball and Onions

During the time the Amanas were a communal society, games like baseball were forbidden by the church elders. However, it didn't take much before word got out about the young Bill Zuber's exceptional athletic skills. When a Cleveland Indians scout showed up to check out the 17-year-old's skills, he found the boy helping with the onion harvest in the kitchen gardens. As the story goes, the scout then picked up an onion (with no baseball around) and asked Bill if he could hit a nearby barn. The young man threw the onion over the barn roof, thus commencing his baseball career. Bill spent six years in the minors, then went on to pitch for 10 years in the majors. When his arm was injured in 1945, he returned home where he and his wife Connie established a restaurant in a hotel built in Homestead in 1862. Although Zuber's Restaurant in Homestead is no longer owned by the Zuber family, today it still retains the name.

In Main Amana, the Colony Inn Restaurant has been around since 1935, as well as the Ox Yoke Inn. The Ox Yoke in particular has long been a favorite of locals who are known to celebrate birthdays and anniversaries here—with good reason (their fresh-baked desserts include some of the best rhubarb pie

Family-style meals fill up everyone in the Amana Colonies.

you'll find anywhere). More-family style fare awaits at the Ronneburg, where the owners are descendants of one of the families that originally lived in the German Ronneburg Castle, the ancestral home of the Amana colonists.

At most of these places, you can plan on ordering fare such as sauerbraten with potato dumplings or a Bavarian Salad of Amana ham, cheese, and beets, served with rye bread. You can also plan on family-style service, with bowls of potatoes, chunks of pickled ham, slices of beets, and coleslaw, all served abundantly. This is hearty food for hearty appetites. (Don't plan on dieting while you're here.)

Also, do take time to tour the Communal Kitchen in Middle Amana; this is the only intact communal-era kitchen remaining in the Amanas, and it's preserved as it appeared in 1932 when the kitchen served community members for the last time. Best of all, your guide could be Marie Calihan, one of those in the kitchens here who originally "lived it and worked it" and can give you a firsthand account of what really went into those meal-making sessions.

Wineries abound in the area as well, and the tradition of Amana winemaking is as old as the villages themselves. During the communal years, Amana vintners in each village made the wine for their community, teaching their offspring the craft. Today, the wineries are each family-owned, with the direct descendents still bottling up and offering visitors tastes of rhubarb, dandelion, elderberry, and a variety of other fruit wines.

It's Because They're Bigger

During Amana's communal years, the punch-ticket system was used to distribute the finished wine. Women were each allowed 12 gallons per year while each man was permitted 20 gallons per year.

Over at the meat market in Main Amana, you can sample the famous smoked Amana hams, plus find Iowa chops, huge breaded pork tenderloins, or thick slabs of smoked bacon. You can also buy small cartons of homespun ham salad. Along with a loaf of bread from Hahn Bakery in Middle Amana (where streusels, coffee cakes, and rolls have been coming out of the original hearth oven since 1866), buy yourself some sweet and spicy home-brewed root beer or cream soda from Millstream Brewery in Amana. Put all your purchases together, and you've got yourself a fine little Amana-style picnic lunch.

Besides all the legendary food here, however, shoppers will find the Amanas well-stocked with handcrafted furniture, clocks, brooms, baskets, lace, quilts, and candles. The Amana Woolen Mill, specializing in wool, cotton, and acrylic blankets, was established in 1857 and is the only operational woolen mill in the state of Iowa today.

Special events and festivities are always going on in the villages too. Happen into the area during June, and you may get in on a tractor parade, when hundreds of vintage tractors circle through Homestead. June is also when the Celebration of Flowers takes place in South Amana, and townsfolk welcome visitors to tour their beautiful home gardens.

Visit in July and you'll find lilies in bloom at Lily Lake, and the fireflies flickering magically around at night. By fall, the harvest season is imminent, with pumpkins heaped on porches and squash taking over gardens.

Whatever the season, though, don't forget to make a visit to Homestead Church. Sitting in the sanctuary, you face the large clear windows that look south over the endless prairie—witnessing much the same timeless vista as those who first chose to settle here.

South Amana

My favorite of the Amana villages, South Amana is the smallest, but it's the most charming. And one of the best times to visit here is in June during the Celebration of Flowers, when local homeowners like Larry and Wilma Rettig open their showcase gardens for visitors to wander through. At the Fern Hill shop in town, the yard is filled with quilts hanging on the clothesline, vintage seeds and plants for sale, and old-world music performances. You can sip a cup of jasmine tea and listen to featured speakers explaining edible blossoms, butterfly gardening, or how to use architectural antiques in the garden.

A Food-Friendly Place To Stay

Baeckerei Bed and Breakfast
507 Q Street
Phone: (319) 622-3597; (800) 391-8650

Truthfully, I can't think of a better place to stay overnight than a bakery. Especially, if it's at Wally and Paula Pasbrig's Baeckerei B&B in South Amana. Built in 1860, this building has the old Amana signature weathered grape trellises lining the outside of its brick walls—and it really was originally South Amana's communal bakery.

Today, it's no longer an operating bakeshop ("Although we do still get people who stop in and ask if there are rolls for sale," says Wally), but staying overnight here almost feels like it could be. Why? It probably has something to do with the morning aromas of cinnamon-y apple French toast and coffee wafting up the stairs. If you stay here, Wally makes guests full breakfasts and serves them at the antique dining room table on the main floor.

Before breakfast, though, a pot of coffee is brought upstairs, and you can sip a cup while relaxing in the sitting room—quiet with only the clock ticking nearby and sunlight easing through the windows. In the bedrooms (there are three), antique accessories like pretty musical powder boxes line the tops of old dressers, and windows look out over cows grazing in faraway fields as well as a butterfly garden below.

If one needs to slow down and decompress from the fast pace of city life, this is the place to stay. And if your car breaks down over in Main Amana, like mine did while I was here, these hosts will no doubt even loan their car to you—like they did for my mom and me. Now, that's real country hospitality.

Rich and wonderful, this breakfast bonanza scents South Amana's Baeckerei Bed and Breakfast on most mornings.

Stuffed French Toast Strata

1 1-pound loaf unsliced French bread
1 8-ounce package cream cheese, cubed
8 eggs
2 1/2 cups milk or half and half
6 tablespoons butter, melted

1/4 cup maple syrup

1 recipe Apple Cider Syrup

Cut French bread into cubes. Spray a 13x9x2-inch baking dish with cooking spray. Place half of the bread cubes in dish. Top with cream cheese cubes. Place the remaining bread cubes on top.

Blend eggs, milk, melted butter, and syrup until well combined. Pour egg mixture evenly over bread. Cover and refrigerate for 2 to 24 hours.

Before baking, remove cover. Bake at 325 degrees for 35 to 40 minutes until center is set. Let stand for 10 minutes. Serve with the Apple Cider Syrup.

Apple Cider Syrup

1/2 cup sugar

4 teaspoons cornstarch

1/2 teaspoon ground cinnamon

1 cup apple cider or apple juice

1 tablespoon lemon juice

2 tablespoons butter

In a small saucepan, stir together the sugar, cornstarch, and cinnamon. Then stir in the apple cider and lemon juice. Cook and stir the mixture over medium heat until mixture is thickened and bubbly. Then cook and stir for two minutes more. Remove saucepan from heat and stir in the butter until it melts.

Accompaniments: Wally serves this with slices of Amana ham, sided with sliced melon, topped with raspberry orange sauce. (Mix seedless raspberry jam and a bit of orange juice together: Keep in squirt bottle for decorating fruit.)

Recipes reprinted by permission of Wally and Paula Pasbrig.

Amana

Ackerman's Winery and Gifts
4406 220 Highway, Phone: (319) 622-3379

Located in Amana (it was originally tucked under a century-old grape arbor in scenic South Amana), Ackerman Winery has been producing quality, award-winning wine for three generations. It has the distinct honor of being the oldest winery operated by one family in the state of Iowa.

Its bright new digs give center stage to the colorful array of gold and pink and purple wines available. These simple country wines are fresh fruit, berry and vegetable variations, reminiscent of grandma and grandpa's farmhouse stash. Dandelion, rhubarb, and elderberry are just a few of the more than 21 varieties made here.

The winery now has a self-guided walk-through tour where you can view the 14,000-gallon wine cellar, observing where the wines are produced, aged, and bottled. Then, if you like, you can sample a few that sound intriguing. Always wondered what cranberry wine tastes like? How about an Iowa Honey version? (It's not bad.) Peach, plum, and raspberry are others, along with a blackberry wine that's outstanding.

Ackerman has also been producing some merlot, Riesling, and chardonnay varieties of wine these days—and they're worth a try.

After you've finished your sampling, check out the gift shop, which features authentic German beer steins, hundreds of wine racks, glasses, and wine accessories.

The Amana Cocktail

In the early days, Concord grape and rhubarb were the only varieties of wine made, and the practice of swirling together a mixture of the two in a glass begat the Amana Cocktail, a drink still popular today.

Ox Yoke Inn
4420 220th Trail, P.O. Box 230
Phone: (319) 622-3441; toll-free reservations
(800) 233-3441

With its cheery, blue-checked tablecloths, authentic beer steins, and spirit of *gemütlichkeit*, it's easy to understand why this place is a favorite (do make reservations) of locals celebrating special occasions as well as visitors touring the colonies.

Originally one of the colonies' communal kitchens, the Ox Yoke was built in 1856. In 1940, William and Lina Leichsenring opened it as the Ox Yoke Inn. (William was born in what is now the Ox Yoke's Amana Dining Room. Lina spent many hours as a young girl working in the kitchen.)

The restaurant's first family-style dinners of fresh meat and vegetables, raised and grown in the Colonies, were served for sixty-five cents! Today, the Ox Yoke Inn tradition is carried on by William and Lina's son William (Bill) Leichsenring, Jr. (he's usually at the main desk greeting and seating folks) and his family—and the price is a bit more than sixty-five cents.

But many of the menu items are still made following the traditional recipes that Lina learned in the communal kitchen. *Wienerschnitzel, sauerbraten,* and *jager schnitzel,* along with barbequed ribs (roasted over six hours) are all part of the sturdy repertoire of favorites served up here—along with those communal bowls of corn, mashed potatoes, cubed ham, and basket of breads from Hahn's hearth oven in Middle Amana. But here's a tip: it's essential to save room for pie, especially if you like rhubarb.

Ox Yoke Inn Rhubarb Custard Pie

3 egg yolks, lightly beaten (at room temperature)

$1/4$ cup half & half

$1^1/2$ cup sugar

1 Tbsp. flour

$1/8$ tsp. salt

4 cups (peeled & cut up) rhubarb

1 unbaked 9" pie shell

Preheat oven to 375 degrees. Mix eggs and cream. Add sugar, flour and salt.

Add rhubarb. Mix thoroughly. Put into the unbaked pie shell. Bake about 1 hour, just until set. (Watch carefully!) When cool, top with your favorite meringue.

Recipe courtesy of William Leichsenring, Jr., and reprinted with permission.

Middle Amana

Hahn Bakery
2510 J Street, Phone: (319) 622-3439

You need to make sure you are at this tidy little shop early, early, if you hope to purchase some of its fresh-from-the-hearth-oven sweet treasures. The hours state 7:30 a.m. until day's baking is sold, and I've arrived here at 9:30 only to find the cinnamon rolls completely gone, and only a few loaves of bread and some cookies left. Do know when you drive up here that the brick building looks like a residence, but go round back (follow those enticing baking smells) and you'll see you're at the right place.

Once inside the cozy shop with its bright blue walls and old wood floors,

Hahn's Hearth Oven Bakery in Middle Amana.

you can even peek in at the wood-fired oven—or if it's not too busy, Doris Hahn will take you round to show you close up.

If you've never tasted bread baked this way, you're in for a treat. There really is nothing like it, with a hard outer crust and an inside rich and dense. Hahn also bakes cinnamon rolls here, and streusel: butter, apricot, and cherry variations all are shaped by hand, exceptional, and meltingly delicious.

Built in 1864, this original wood-fired stone hearth is 10 feet wide, 10 feet deep, and holds 140 loaves of bread at one time. It's designed to be heated with a wood fire set in the baking chamber, preheating the brick interior; since 1985 natural gas has been used to heat the oven. There is no flame during baking—only the heat retained in the brick. One heating allows Hahn to bake up to 350 items—which, of course, includes those hard-crusted breads, coffeecakes, and streusels. They take about two hours to bake this way.

For years, Doris Hahn and her late husband Jack were a team in the kitchen, beginning at 1:30 a.m. with their bread mixing and baking. Today, Hahn is still baking and turning out these made-with-love goods.

Don't miss a stop here.

Kelly Roberson's 10 Iowa Food Favorites

Kelly Roberson is the editor of *The Iowan* and *Iowa Gardening* magazines.

1. Any place that serves Sheeder Farms beef, chicken, or eggs

2. Any place that serves Niman Ranch bacon. Pork the way it should be

3. Hamburg Inn, Iowa City. Funky place, great hamburger fare, iconoclastic place

4. Snookies, Des Moines. I love old-school ice cream places, and this is a classic, with a drive-up window and puppy cones too.

5. Any of the re-creation dinners at Living History Farms. Old-style food that is incomparable for the experience

6. The Lincoln Café, Mount Vernon. An unexpected find

7. Great Plains Pizza, Ames. College atmosphere, a classic visit

8. Iowa State Fair. One of the best reasons to go to the fair is the food—no matter what your inclination.

9. Taylor's Maid-Rite, Marshalltown. Serves the classic loose-meat sandwich.

10. Thai Flavors, Des Moines. Fresh ingredients, incomparable Thai food.

DeWitt

Sunrise Family Restaurant
906 Sixth Avenue, Phone: (563) 659-9476

Get to the Sunrise early on Sunday mornings if you want to beat the church crowd. This eat-off-the-floor clean spot packs in the people—dressed up families waving hi to grandkids, and friends circling tables greeting each other. This is the kind of down-home place where waitresses call you "hon" and respond "sure thing, sweetie," when you ask for an extra spoon. The owner dashes through the room often, a pot of coffee in each hand (regular and decaf), expertly filling up coffee cups a couple times or more.

The menu is billed as "Oriental-American Cuisine," but between the burgers, hot gravy plates, ravioli, gyros, and chicken breasts, I would have to say I did not find anything remotely "oriental" to order.

But it doesn't matter, because what you want to eat here is breakfast. More specifically, the corned beef hash served with a couple eggs and homemade raisin bread (yes, toasted please). This is hash made the way it should be: diced, shredded corned beef tossed into potatoes—arriving a crisp, soft, mildly spicy combo of flavor, textures, and scent. With perfectly cooked eggs and toast, it's a breakfast to remember.

In the Pumpkin Spirit: Anamosa's Pumpkinfest

Proclaimed the Pumpkin Capital of Iowa, Anamosa celebrates its status annually during the first weekend in October.

That's when Pumpkinfest and the Ryan Norlin Memorial Great Pumpkin Weigh-Off takes place. One of 20 North American sites for the Great Pumpkin Commonwealth Weigh-Off, this competition is not taken lightly. The top three prizes range from $500 to $1,500. Prize-winning pumpkins have been tipping the scales at well over 1,000 pounds—with a recent winner's entry weighing in at 1,159 pounds!

Besides pumpkins, there are also categories and competition in cantaloupe, tomatoes, gourds, and watermelon. Other pumpkin-related activities at the festival include a pumpkin parade, pumpkin toss, pumpkin-carving display, and, of course, a pumpkin recipe contest. A Sunday morning pumpkin-pancake breakfast caps off the weekend.

Cedar Rapids

Sykora Bakery
73 16th Avenue SW, Phone: (319) 364-5271

It's hard to resist a stop into this beloved neighborhood bakery. Even from the sidewalk, you can smell the sweet aromas seeping out the door here.

Inside, the first thing you see is the glass bakery display case showing off dozens of the Czech delight known as *kolache* (spelled a million different ways). If you look closely, you'll also notice the word *kolache* etched into the glass. Behind, the open-faced fruit-filled little treats include garden-fresh rhubarb (my favorite), raspberry, pineapple, apple, cherry, apricot, blueberry, pear, as well as the traditional poppy seed (not my favorite) and prune (definitely not my favorite).

This always-bustling bakery in the Czech Village is a true treasure. Steeped in history, its worn wood floors and lace-curtained windows date back to 1900. First used as a beer bottling plant, it became the C. K. Kosek Bakery in 1903 and Sykora in 1927. Today, it's owned and being restored by John and Susan

Rocarek. They've already begun work on replacing the storefront's tall wood facade that once faced the street.

John and Susan live in the neighborhood, only four blocks away, and John (a full-blooded Czech) grew up living only five blocks from the shop. His childhood memories include many visits to the bakery, especially for his addiction: *rohliky* (a crescent-shaped sweet dough pastry). They still make the sweet today, but you need to get here early in the morning to be assured you'll get some. They've also been updating cake and cookie recipes, but one recipe they've kept constant is the *kolaches*. George, the baker here since he was 13, is a cousin of the original Sykora family—and is making sure of that.

This big store is crammed full of great stuff. Breads (try the Bohemian rye) are showcased against one wall, pans of raspberry bars and pastries fill another display. On the counter you can even buy Almond Bark Dog Treats (bone-shaped cookies) for your pet. The opposite side of the room is crowded with several table-clothed round ice cream tables for two and chairs. A mannequin in the window is dressed in an authentic Czech outfit. Shelves with day-old bakery are next to shelves displaying books about Prague and *Czechoslovak Wit and Wisdom*. A high chair is nearby if you've brought baby—and in keeping with the times there's also a coffee bar now, serving up espresso and lattes.

Zindricks Czech Restaurant
86 16th Avenue SW, Phone: (319) 365-5257

Eating at Zindricks feels kind of like dining at an old-fashioned supper club. Booths line one wall, tables fill the middle, and there's a free-standing fireplace in the middle, filled with numerous green plants. There are paper placemats and

One of several restaurants in the Czech Village, Cedar Rapids.

pretty water goblets, silverware wrapped in white linen, and lovely, polite waitresses. Meals are served with all sorts of choices: potato or bread dumplings (choose the potato ones), sauerkraut or sweet and sour cabbage, home-style chunky applesauce sprinkled with cinnamon, and rye bread.

The menu is a blend of Czech and American favorites, but let's face it, it's the Czech specialties that really shine here. Not to mention, where else are you going to see liver dumpling soup on the menu?

Cabbage rolls are dense with ground chuck and rice, a whiff of clove, all packaged in cabbage leaves before being baked in Zindrick's fine tomato sauce to a bubbling finish. The slow-roasted pork loin is lush and tender—in a gravy that simply sings of home. The *pierogis* are stuffed with your choice of filling: chicken with mozzarella, pork with sauerkraut and caraway Swiss, or beef with sautéed onion and green pepper. Choice of sauces includes an orange-y fragrant paprika sauce.

For dessert, the waitress brings around a little glass plate with offerings like lemon layer cake (good) blueberry crepes (better), or cherry strudel (best).

Do check out the bathrooms here—they are spotlessly clean and feel like you're at your grandma's. On the women's counter by the sink, there's hairspray, lotion, and even mouthwash.

Little Bohemia Tavern
1317 Third Street SE, Phone: (319) 364-9396

It's a few blocks from most of the Czech Village shops and eateries, but Little Bohemia Tavern is a place everybody you speak with in the area will advise you to visit. Even if you skip its Czech goulash (you can smell its hearty aroma as soon as you park the car nearby), you must at least peek into this great old building. Listed on the National Register of Historic Places, it's filled with Cedar Rapids memorabilia (including another Czech-dressed mannequin up front) and photos. The old bar looks like it's been here forever—and you wonder what spirits linger in a place with so much history. Oilcloth-covered tables fill half of the well-kept room, and the food here is simple and good.

Polehna's Meat Market
96 16th Avenue SW, Phone: (319) 362-2159

Located in the heart of Cedar Rapids' nationally known Czech Village, this family-run meat market has been in business since 1931 (its awning proclaims it as Cedar Rapids' oldest meat market as well). Besides hand cutting and trimming all meats, they use a genuine wood-burning smokehouse.

A heavy but cheery bright red screen door opens and closes constantly as the parade of customers moves in and out picking up Iowa-cut pork chops, New York strips, and country-style ribs. But the real reason most people shop here is for the Czech specialties made from authentic Czech recipes. This is the place to purchase homemade ring bologna, bratwurst, summer sausage, and wieners with a spicy bite. You'll also find Czech-style potato dumplings, blood sausage (*jelita*), liver sausage (*jitrnice*), head cheese, pork ears, and even pickled pigs' feet! Regulars come on Saturdays for the ham loaf—it's actually a meat loaf—and there's nothing quite like it. The woman standing next to me told me that once it's cooked and sliced and sandwiched between bread, it's the best. (Unfortunately, it also sells out quickly—but call ahead and they'll save you some.).

The small store is earthy and aromatic, filled with laughter and neighbors who obviously have known each other for years. A collection of pig paraphernalia fills the one display window, while two chairs and a table strewn with coloring books and crayons fill the other. It's definitely a family place, run by folks whose pride and caring shine through.

Cookies from Quaker Oats

Cedar Rapids is home to the world's largest cereal mill, owned by Quaker Oats. Here is the original recipe that the company first printed on its Quaker Oats package in 1955—it's still popular today.

Famous Oatmeal Cookies

1 cup firmly packed brown sugar

3/4 cup vegetable shortening

1/2 cup granulated sugar

1 egg

1/4 cup water

1 teaspoon vanilla

3 cups Quaker Oats (Quick or Old Fashioned, uncooked)

1 cup all-purpose flour

1 teaspoon salt (optional)

1/2 teaspoon baking soda

1. Heat oven to 350 degrees. In large bowl, beat brown sugar, shortening, and granulated sugar until creamy. Add egg, water, and vanilla; beat well. Add combined oats, flour, salt, and baking soda; mix well.

2. Drop dough by rounded teaspoonfuls onto ungreased cookie sheets.

3. Bake 11 to 13 minutes or until edges are golden brown. Remove to wire rack. Cool completely. Store tightly covered.

Variation
Add 1 cup of any one or a combination of any of the following ingredients to basic cookie dough: raisins, chopped nuts, chocolate chips, or shredded coconut.

Large Cookies
Drop by rounded tablespoonfuls onto ungreased cookie sheets. Bake 15 to 17 minutes. About 2$^1/2$ dozen.
  Recipe courtesy of The Quaker Oats Company and reprinted with permission.

Iowa City

Sanctuary Restaurant and Pub
405 South Gilbert, Phone: (319) 351-5692

A neighborhood and local favorite, this tavern-like place has an old-world, dark interior with a relaxed and bohemian atmosphere.

Established in 1972, the place offers much more than nondescript pub grub, though. Appetizers feature mussels steamed in Belgian ale, crab cakes, and a dynamite Thai basil chicken—bite-size pieces of chicken skewered and then covered with spicy fresh basil sauce. Entrees, which come with home-baked garlicky bread, include Cajun stew with andouille sausage and tuna topped with a gingered mango sauce. Still, pizzas are probably the most popular item on the menu—a thin, crispy crust piled high with all kinds of good stuff sets them apart. Try the Pizza Pimienta—cilantro pesto, roasted red peppers, jalapenos, and cheese. Especially great with a beer.

Speaking of. You definitely should have a brewski here. With its astounding selection of international beers, you can get everything from a Belgium Augustijn (an amber ale first brewed from this same recipe in 1295, according to the menu) to an English classic called Old Peculiar. It's an education just reading the descriptions.

New Pioneer Co-op
22 South Van Buren Street, Phone: (319) 338-9441

If you don't have time or can't get out to the local orchards, farmers' markets, or berry farms, this food shop is a super place to pick up fresh produce. Springtime, freshly picked asparagus starts arriving from **Buchanan Farm and Earth Preserve**. In May, lettuces and snow peas begin showing up from the **Friendly**

Farm. Mid-summer, you'll find baskets of homegrown blueberries from **Bock Berry Farm** and strawberries from **Scattergood School Farm**. In July, shelves are loaded with zucchinis, green beans, cukes, cabbages, eggplant, kale, Swiss chard, onions, and cilantro.

By harvest time, locals are anxiously awaiting Janette Ryan-Busch's red and green bell peppers and fresh basil from **Fae Ridge Farm**. Of course, when sweet corn and tomatoes are ready, they arrive in colorful abundance, along with the rest of autumn's bounty: melons from Neuzil's and apples and prize-winning cider (this one sells out fast) from **Sand Road Orchard**.

A full-line grocery store, the Co-op has lots of other great buys and offerings—bulk spices and coffees, organic cream cheese and butter, fresh bakery, meats, grains, cheeses, seafood, and even wines.

Hamburg Inn No. 2
214 North Linn Street, Phone: (319) 337-5512

Hamburgers sizzled on the grill and served on a warm bun, accompanied by some crispy Brew City onion rings and a shake, makes the meal at the Hamburg Inn No. 2. (No. 1 is long gone.) Since 1948, this eat shack has been dishing up "comfort food in a fifties time capsule." Breakfasts are legendary too, but it's the juicy, hand-pattied burgers that reign supreme. Bizarre combos include a Loco Burger (served with a hard egg), a Hula Burger (topped with Swiss cheese and pineapple), a Teriyaki Burger (smothered in the sauce, with green peppers), and a Reuben Burger (Swiss and sauerkraut).

Wood booths and a black painted pressed-tin ceiling add to the place's retro allure—as well as the fact that here when you order a malt you get what's left over in the tin container too. It's basically like getting two for the price of one. Malts and shakes come in all flavors: coffee, lemon, maple, cherry, chocolate, blueberry. Or you can try something truly weird called a Pie Shake—a piece of pie smushed into the ice cream and blended like a shake. It was written up in the *New York Times*—although I have yet to meet a local who has ordered one.

In 1933, during the depths of the Great Depression, Iowa City had 41 family-owned grocery stores. Today, John's Grocery is the only one remaining.

John's Grocery, Inc.
401 East Market Street, Phone: (319) 337-2183

This corner mom-and-pop grocery store built in 1848 is the last of its kind. Or maybe it's the first of its kind. It's certainly one of a kind. It's also a well-loved institution in Iowa City. The parking lot is crappy and the store is cramped. But the place oozes with heart and soul. Express an interest in the building and one of the staff here is likely to proudly take you on a tour—showing off the curved ceiling of the "cave" in the basement, along with sharing the amazing history that goes with it.

The deli is stocked with artisanal cheeses from France, Italy, and Belgium—even including two from Trappist monasteries. Fresh-daily baked breads and buns (e.g., white, wheat, rye, cheese, tomato, Parmesan basil, dill, Italian herb) scent the room along with sweet aromas of cookies (molasses, snickerdoodles—yum!), cinnamon rolls (do NOT miss these), pies, pastries, bars, and brownies.

John's also stocks meats, sandwich fixin's, salads, and a superb selection of bottled microbrewed root beers and cream sodas.

But once you start strolling through the various little rooms here, you'll realize why the folks whom you asked for directions here wondered if you were looking for John's Beer Store instead of John's Grocery.

John's is, quite frankly, a beer aficionado's dream come true. One of the rooms you step into is literally loaded with everything from six-packs of Miller Lite to 15-year-old bottles of ale found in the basement of a London liquor store. Their ad boasts around 700 specialty, craft-brewed, and imported beers—representing at least 30 different countries. You can choose beers from Argentina to Viet Nam, but most notable are the bottles from Germany, Czech Republic, Britain, Ireland, and Scotland. John's is also one of the most diverse outlets for Belgian beer "on this continent"—with more than 125 to select from. Specialty domestic microbrews number at least 175, in the store at any point in time, and microbrews include rotating seasonal ones. In other words, there's always something new to find.

Besides its beer, John's wine offerings are numerous too. John's also carries what they label "breweriana" in another room—or an annex, actually. Here's where to find things like a Guinness Black and Tan spoon (for making the perfect Black and Tan, of course), and all sorts of beer glasses. From boots to flutes, snifters and tulips (considered the best vessels to "nose" an especially aromatic beer), steins and krugs (those lids used to have a reason—to keep the flies out of your beer), as well as the plain old pilsner glasses. Who knew there were so many wonderful ways to enjoy drinking beer?? This is way beyond a keg and a plastic cup.

Tasty tenderloins are served everywhere in Iowa.

Tenderloin: An Iowa Favorite

Iowans love their pork tenderloin, and they have a few rules about the right way to eat it, according to Bob Modersohn, who wrote about Iowa's tasty tenderloins for the *Des Moines Register*:

- The classic pork tenderloin normally is served overlapping a regular size hamburger (or kaiser) bun, topped with mustard, ketchup, onion, and pickles.
- Prices generally start at $3.50; $6 is tops.
- It's okay to have it cut in half.

As part of that 2004 story, Modersohn also asked readers to send in their favorite places to eat a tenderloin. Here are the results.

In Des Moines

Smitty's Tenderloin Shop, 1401 Army Post Road

Michael's Restaurant and Lounge, 4041 Urbandale Avenue

George the Chili King, 5722 Hickman Road

Outside Des Moines

Shack's Lounge, Bayard

CJ's, Aspinwall

Community Tavern, Fort Dodge

Coon River Bar and Grill, Van Meter

Crouse's Cafe, Indianola

Dairy Sweet, Dunlap

Darrell's Place, Hamlin

Horseshoe Lanes Grill, Adel

Jewel's Food and Spirits, Troy Mills

Jo's Bar and Grill, Searsboro

Joensy's, Center Point

McNamara Café, Prairieburg

MC Café, Martinsburg

Niland's Café, Colo

Peru Tap, Peru

Pork and More, Albion

Red Barn, Exira

Red Rooster, Iowa Falls

St. Olaf Tavern, St. Olaf (northeast Iowa)

S&J Roadside Bar & Grill, Floris

Smitty's, Albia

Suburban Restaurant, Gilbert
Reprinted by permission of the Des Moines Register.

Kalona

Kalona Cheese Factory
2206 540th Street SW, Phone: (319) 656-2776

This always-busy shop is crowded and jam-packed. There's no doubt it's the remarkable selection of cheeses for sale here—more than two hundred imported and domestic varieties—that brings customers in. But the shop is about much more than cheese. Offering a little bit of everything, it's a perfect place to pick up goods for a picnic if you happen to be road tripping. Check out the rainbow-hued jars of Amish fruit spreads: strawberry-rhubarb, blueberry, apricot, blackberry—plus an assortment of gourmet goods: mustards, syrups, salad dressings, sausages, cookies, and crackers. Meats from the nearby Brighton Locker include pork patties, bratwurst, summer sausage, and beef sticks.

While you're here, you can also watch the cheese-making process through observation windows. (Only the white cheddar is made on the premises.) The white cheddar cheese curds (the kind that squeak when you bite into them) are made fresh daily. For the record, it's a rare soul who leaves the shop without at least one bag of these tasty morsels.

Columns & Chocolate
212 Fourth Street, Phone: (319) 656- 2992

Originally a home, this grand old mansion now turned tea room, gift shop, and bed and breakfast dates back to the early 1900s, and even sports a fairy-tale-style turret. On the main floor, several light-filled rooms are filled with mismatched antique chairs and tables covered with chintz, along with an eclectic mix of gifts that women are always on the look-out for their sisters, girlfriends, moms, or special aunties.

You can wander the rooms admiring walls decorated with vintage valentines as wallpaper, or teapots of every shape and pattern lined up on a shelf, then decide where you want to sit for lunch. The menu is small and generally features two entrees—lovely, delicately rich things, e.g., country ham and broccoli in a creamy cheese sauce, poured over a crepe, drizzled with a pretty squiggle and zip of raspberry honey mustard—or, if you've brought the mister, a hearty grilled chicken sandwich slathered with farmhouse chutney and a cream cheese spread.

If you're here later in the afternoon, this is a pleasantly civilized spot for a glass of, say, raspberry quince iced tea and dessert. Fresh from the oven, there are always a good half dozen sweets to choose from (although they do sell out early): bread pudding with warm vanilla sauce, three-berry cobbler baked in a tea cup, a dinner-plate-size brown sugar cookie, or a slice of deluxe fudge cake . . . with lots of whipped cream.

Wilton

The Wilton Candy Kitchen
310 Cedar Street, Phone: (563) 732-2278

Here it is, the vintage soda fountain ice cream experience you've been dreaming about. Even from the outside, the Candy Kitchen looks like it did decades ago with its red-and-white striped awnings and bright red door. Entering the shop is like discovering yourself in an old black-and-white photo that's become a color print. Truly, the place today looks almost the same as it did in the sepia-toned photographs from the 1920s. Walnut booths trimmed in marble and glass, gorgeous mirrors, leaded-glass lamp shades over each booth, an intricately designed stamped metal ceiling—and, of course, the piece de resistance, the old marble soda fountain.

Housed in an 1865 building, the shop is listed on the National Register of Historic Places, and according to co-owner Thelma Nopoulos it's "the oldest ongoing ice cream parlor/soda fountain in the world."

What's more all-American than a banana split from the Wilton Candy Kitchen?

Know right off that decision-challenged folks at this place are in trouble. Lots of choices to consider: starting out with simply where to sit? At the marble counter where you can watch George scoop the ice cream out of the freezers and put together dazzling sodas? Or over at one of those lovely old booths? And if a booth, then how about the one where Gregory Peck once sat and ordered what's now become the Gregory Peck Special: Grilled Cheese and a Chocolate Soda?

After that decision is made, there's the next dilemma. If it's lunchtime, what to eat? An old-fashioned ham salad sandwich, or a light turkey and cheese? On white bread or whole wheat? Toasted or not? How about an iced phosphate to wash it all down? Choices include vanilla, cherry, strawberry, orange, or the classic Green River-lemon-lime phosphate. Then again, are you sure you might not want a Red River-strawberry and cherry phosphate?

Next, it's on to the final and most important decision of all. What kind of ice cream treat—made with George's homemade ice cream—are you going to indulge in? A summery strawberry sundae, topped with fresh-from-the-garden strawberries? How 'bout a chocolate soda made with George's own secret recipe of chocolate syrup? A malt

Don't miss a stop at the Wilton Candy Kitchen in Wilton.

buzzed up with butterscotch? Creamy and decadent, it's too thick for a straw. The list goes on . . .

After you've finished your meal, and if you have time, it's fun to take a look round the museum in the back room of the store. Filled with the Candy Kitchen and town's history, it's a labor of love filled with memorabilia.

Since 1940, George and Thelma Nopoulos have been operating this sweet business founded by George's father. But both will tell you that they have been working in the shop here much longer than that. Truth be told, George says his first job, at age six, was to stand on a wire ice cream chair and wind the Brunswick record player.

Thelma Soteros Nopoulos, whose father was a fellow Greek immigrant, was washing dishes here in the Candy Kitchen at age 10. As for meeting and marrying George, she says, what do you expect when you have two fathers from Greece playing matchmaker?

The two continue to mind their store seven days a week, serving up George's homemade ice cream, putting together soda fountain delights, and sharing their wonderful hometown hospitality every moment.

Indeed. "George wakes up at 5, waiting for 7 to go to work," says Thelma.

Soda Fountain Memories

"After he showed us how he used to make a cherry coke at his dad's soda fountain in California, he put his arm around me and gave me a kiss on the cheek and I don't remember what happened after. I blacked out," says Thelma, recalling Gregory Peck's visit to the Wilton Candy Kitchen.

The American Dream

On June 10, 1910, 10,000 miles from his hometown in Greece, Gus G. Nopoulos started living the American dream as he reopened the doors of the Candy Kitchen in Wilton. Little did he know that first day that the doors would stay open seven days a week, 365 days a year for the next 92 years. That first day, William Howard Taft was president of the United States, women couldn't vote, and the Wright Brothers were still trying to sell their first airplane to the United States Army.

Seventeen dollars was tabulated at the cash register that first day (a good thing, since the rent for the building was eight dollars a month...pretty steep for a new business), not bad for a man who knew only two words of English, "Thank you," and whose only asset

was the ability to work 16 to 18 hours a day, seven days a week.
*Courtesy of George and Thelma Nopoulos and reprinted with
permission from their shop's advertising pamphlet.*

Lori Erickson's 10 Iowa Food Favorites

Lori Erickson is a freelance writer in Iowa City and author of *Iowa:
Off the Beaten Path* and *Sweet Corn and Sushi: The Story of Iowa and
Yamanashi.*

Breitbach's Country Dining, Balltown. The state's best
homemade pies and a lovely view of the Mississippi River Valley.
Don't miss the vintage mural in the bar.

Lincoln Café, Mount Vernon. This small town north of Iowa
City has one of the country's finest restaurants. Go figure.

The Machine Shed, Urbandale and Davenport. Iowa food at
its best. Massive servings of meat and potatoes, expertly prepared.
Just don't bother taking your vegetarian friends there.

John's Grocery, Iowa City. An old-fashioned corner market with
an astonishingly good beer and wine selection. They love to give
advice on what goes best with dinner.

Jacob's Table and Market, Postville. A kosher Jewish deli and
restaurant in a small Iowa town. The market stocks classics like
corned beef, pastrami, lox, bagels, and challah. At the restaurant,
try the turkey shwarma.

Bricktown, Dubuque. A fine microbrewery and restaurant
housed in a historic building in downtown Dubuque.

Liz Clark's, Keokuk. Dining by reservation only in the
Italianate mansion of one of the Midwest's finest chefs.

Kin Folks Eatin' Place, Attica. Terrific slow-cooked barbeque. Ask
about the restaurant's connection to the comedian Roseanne Barr.

Columns & Chocolate, Kalona. A delightful café in a funky
older home. Like being at your grandmother's, if you were lucky
enough to have an exceedingly cool grandmother.

New Pioneer Co-op, Iowa City. The mother lode for organic
foods, fine wines, and gourmet cheeses in the Midwest.

The Great River Road

Pig Roasts and Friday Night Fish Fries

Of all the regions in Iowa, I'd have to say the area around the Great River Road remains my favorite. Driving through small river towns edged between bluffs and the waters of the Mississippi River, I love seeing friendly folks wave from front porch swings, or a sign by the local American Legion promoting a "Pork Chop Dinner and Bake Sale."

Following roads lined with wildflowers and coming upon the occasional mailbox painted and shaped like a corn stalk are part of the area's simple pleasures and small joys. Of course, along the roads that curve and follow the river, you'll also find good old-fashioned eating establishments: steakhouses and supper clubs, pig roasts and Friday night fish fries—as timeless and treasured as the river they overlook.

There's no better place to start out a drive on the GRR that combines such pleasures than in Lansing, a few miles south of the Minnesota border. Stop in to the Model Bakery for a bag of doughnuts, then head to Mount Hosmer Park, where the inspiring river view is one of the best.

Leaving Lansing heading south takes you through a beautiful portion of the state often referred to as the "little Switzerland of Iowa"—for obvious reasons.

A view of the Mississippi from Iowa's Great River Road.

A few miles before Harpers Ferry, the scenic river road passes by the tiny Wexford Immaculate Conception Church. Covered in ivy, high atop a hill with a small country cemetery surrounding it, it's a setting right out of a movie.

A few miles north of Marquette is Effigy Mounds National Monument—a beautiful preserve spread along the Mississippi River bluffs. (Don't plan an alfresco luncheon here, though; these are considered sacred grounds and no picnicking is allowed.) From here, the road winds its way into Marquette, a workaday town with a can't-miss pink elephant riverboat casino, and McGregor, a gem of a small river town with antique shops tucked along the restored Main Street.

Overnight at McGregor's Little Switzerland Inn and from the upstairs porch you can see the Mississippi River across the street. On a warm evening, plan to take a stroll from the inn to the Beer & Bratz Garden—and sit on its deck area, within touching distance of the river.

Two miles southeast of McGregor on Highway 340, make a stop at Pike's Peak State Park. Here you can stand on one of the highest points along the entire Mississippi, a 500-foot bluff overlooking the meeting of Mississippi and Wisconsin Rivers. Nearby hiking trails and picnic spots abound—plan ahead for taking a mid-morning coffee break or picnic lunch here.

Afterward, the road makes its way past pale, sun-soaked cornfields and (in the autumn) gorgeous color-splashed trees, into lovely Guttenberg. Lined with stone and brick buildings of the 1840s, Guttenberg's riverfront parallels the river with a great-for-strolling river walk.

Out of Guttenberg, the river road follows along above the river valley. At Turkey River Indian Mounds, County Road C96, also known as the Balltown Road, takes you into Dubuque. Traversing through rolling fields, with the glimmering Mississippi in the distance, the road winds and dips through farmscapes and some of the most classic country vistas you'll ever experience. I'd have to say it is one of my all-time favorite stretches of road to travel in the entire country.

In Balltown—"achoo" and you're through it—you can't miss the building housing Breitbach's Country Dining; and a stop here is a tradition with many on their annual leaf-peeping excursions.

Dubuque has become a sprawling city, with its share of fast food franchises and chain hotels. But it's still not hard to find old-fashioned favorites either, places like Mario's Italian Restaurant. Or Timmerman's Supper Club in East Dubuque, which is actually in Illinois. Be sure to get a window seat here at sunset for a meal with a view across the river into Iowa.

Closer to the water, you'll find Dubuque's historic Old Main District being revamped with some exceptional food places such as Café Manna Java, Bricktown Brewery & Grill, and the popular Pepper Sprout restaurant. Not far away is Dubuque's newest project: a $188 million educational, entertainment and historic riverfront development featuring a National Mississippi River

Museum and Aquarium as well as a water park, river walk, and conference center.

South from Dubuque, the land is interspersed with country churches, tranquil silent cemeteries, and quaint little villages. In St. Donatus, I always take a brief detour from town, driving a short way east up the hill to the Saint Donatus Catholic Church. Built in 1858 and restored in 1907, the gray limestone building is surrounded by a cemetery with mossy, historic old stones and markers, many bearing inscriptions in French and German. One of my favorite things to do here is to sit on the front steps of the church and look out across the rolling fields to the twin spires of the German Lutheran St. John's church across the way. It's a classic country vista, one of those settings that simply transcends time.

The next town is Bellevue, and this is where the GRR returns to the Mississippi River, with a lengthy Main Street and Riverfront Park alongside Lock and Dam Number 12. Bellevue is another lovely river town, with several historic homes that double as bed and breakfasts offering country hospitality, great desserts, and grand views of the Mississippi River.

From Bellevue, the Iowa River Road leads you first through Clinton, and then into Le Claire, birthplace and childhood home of Buffalo Bill Cody (check out the Faithful Pilot if it's time for lunch). From Le Claire, the River Road heads on to the metropolitan area known as the Quad Cities. The Quad Cities is actually a misnomer, as there are five cities that come together here on the river: Bettendorf and Davenport in Iowa, and Rock Island, Moline, and East Moline in Illinois.

Davenport's Museum of Art is always on my list to visit, and shopping and strolling the Victorian-era village of East Davenport is fun too. Nearby, you'll see brick-paved streets and magnificent nineteenth-century mansions sporting verandahs and turrets. A stop at Lagomarcino's for a hot fudge sundae is a must in the village. But for the real deal in soda fountain ambiance (dark mahogany booths, octagon-tiled floor, hand-dipped chocolates), you really should drive next door to Moline where the original Lagomarcino's 1908 ice cream shop is still located.

McGregor

Twisted Chicken
212 South Main Street, Phone: (563) 873-1515

The ambiance at the Twisted Chicken seems to be one of artful sophistication, more apropos of a big-city dining establishment than a small river-town eatery. But the place is certainly not pretentious. After all, with a name like the Twisted Chicken, you know the owners have a sense of humor to go along with such classy surroundings.

Located on McGregor's charming Main Street, the place started out as an inn (there are two contemporary suites upstairs for rent), evolved into a coffeehouse, and finally blossomed into a full-scale restaurant in 2002. Owners Neil Rettig and Kim Hayes fell in love with the McGregor area on an autumn visit in 1985 and when an opportunity arose for them to move here, they didn't pass it up.

Walls of deep cranberry are perfect backdrops for local artwork displays (changed four times a year) and the silver pressed-tin ceiling shines high overhead in this historic space—while two bay windows on the main level overlook Main Street.

But it's the food that surprises and surpasses small-town expectations here. Okay, it's a bit pricey by local standards, and you probably wouldn't want to check in with the family in tow. But for diners wanting to share a gourmet meal, a bottle of good wine, and conversation, nothing else can match this place for miles.

The chef, Tom Griffin, a friend of the owners', was leaving another job when he joined in the renovation efforts of the Twisted Chicken. A traditionally French-trained chef, it's easy to see that his excellence and simplicity are what keeps the half dozen constantly changing entrees all worthwhile. He uses local and organic produce, daily-fresh seafood, dry-aged Angus beef, and pasture-raised Berkshire pork. "Nothing's from a can here. It's all from scratch and it's fresh," our waitress informed us.

One night, you might get lucky with a blue-cheesy-sauced chicken breast tossed with spinach fettuccine—or a char-broiled sugar-cured salmon with a dollop of fresh chilled cucumber puree smoothed over. Soups like a potato and portabella chowder are unusual and lovely. Service is small-town friendly but professional.

Tip: This is a beautiful autumn drive destination—and for a weekend getaway, plan to reserve (call several weeks ahead) one of the two suites upstairs. Added bonus? You're assured freshly ground coffee or espresso in the morning (not always easy to find in small river towns).

Why "Twisted Chicken"?

In 1988, Neil Rettig and Kim Hayes, future owners of the Twisted Chicken, moved to Prairie du Chien, Wisconsin, after purchasing a very picturesque but defunct farm. Among the somewhat rundown outbuildings was a chicken coop. They decided to get a bunch of laying hens and have fresh eggs.

They picked out 50 assorted hens from a mail-order hatchery and put in their order. Not long after, they received the day-old chicks and proceeded to raise them "by the book." When the hens were about two weeks old they noticed that six or seven of the chicks had dowager's humps and were bent and twisted. Some even walked sideways.

Questioning their "by the book" methods, the two wondered what they might be doing wrong to have caused this physical aberration. However, after a thorough orthopedic exam, they decided nothing was broken and declared them "healthy, but twisted."

The hens proceeded to live normal lives, clustering together, seeming to know that they were special—someday to be famous. As a group they roamed freely through the yard—eating, sunning themselves, and dust bathing. They wandered in and out of the hen house like normal chickens.

One day while referring to the hens, Neil called them "The Twisted Chickens." The name stuck. Eventually they all passed on to roam the Big Free-Range Farm in the Sky, leaving only fond memories.

Years later when it came time to pick a name for their restaurant, Neil and Kim recalled their "Twisted Chickens"—and decided it was an unusual name that folks would remember.

Reprinted with permission from www.Thetwistedchicken.com

White Springs Supper Club
30165 Klein Brewery Road, Phone: (563) 873-9642

This has to be the quintessential supper club—a one-of-a-kind place that really should be a mandatory stop for all those road food aficionados looking for the real deal. Located on the west end of town (on the former site of the Klein Brewery), the building is always packed with people. The scent of hickory-smoked ribs (the smoking is done on the premises), along with constant noisy chatter and laughter of neighbors greeting neighbors fills the place with a happy homespun spirit. You can't go wrong ordering steak with hand-peeled, honest to goodness, mashed potatoes—or the unforgettable smoked ribs and homemade potato salad. Then again, the battered-lightly, fried-crispy catfish prepared here is considered by some to be the best in the world.

Guttenberg

Café Mississippi
431 South River Park Drive, Phone: (563) 252-4405

It's not necessarily for the basic menu of sandwiches or dinners that I recommend a visit to this place; it's for the view that goes with your meal. This place is right on the water—with a wall of windows and complimentary binoculars hanging nearby for folks to use. Overlooking Lock and Dam Number 10 on the Mississippi, the place is popular with locals. (Our server informed us that the Breitbachs from nearby Balltown had eaten here the night before, which is not a significant bit of news in itself until you realize that the Breitbach family owns one of the oldest and most respected restaurants in the state.) So, reservations on busy summer evenings are a good idea.

But, back to those sandwiches: Where else can you find a pork tenderloin for $3.75? Or a super deluxe eight-ounce hunk of ground beef smothered in grilled onions and melt-y cheese on rye bread for the same? How 'bout that baked ham sandwich for $2.50? The most expensive sandwich on the menu could also be the most popular item on the menu: the Rueben. At $4.25 it's a classic of sliced corned beef layered with sauerkraut and Swiss cheese. Dinners run about $10 to $15. Don't miss the all-you-can-eat Friday night cod and catfish special, or Saturday night's prime rib deal. Breakfast is nice here too.

German Fest
Fourth Weekend of September

When the river breezes are cool with that evocative scent of autumn, it's time for this town to celebrate its German heritage. Held in the downtown historic district, Friday night is the Hog Roast, Saturday there's a pancake breakfast at the school, and all day there's music—from accordion melodies to yodeling to polka bands.

Of course, it wouldn't be a German Fest without a beer tent and some grilled brats. Those looking for more German fare head over to the Kanndle Lounge where a German-style buffet features plenty of marinated pot roast, hot bacon-y German potato salad, and red cabbage with apples.

Balltown

Breitbach's Country Dining
563 Balltown Road, Phone: (563) 552-2220

Opened in 1852 (and operated by the Breitbach family since 1891), a sign out front boasts it's "Iowa's Oldest Bar And Restaurant"—and if for no other reason than that, you must stop. Outside, there are wagon wheels leaning against the building and old farm implements displayed. Inside, the rooms are loaded with antique tables, mismatched chairs, lanterns, quilts, and

You can't miss Breitbach's Country Dining establishment in Balltown.

country memorabilia. Heck, there's even a horse blanket supposedly left behind after a visit by the outlaw Jesse James and his gang. (This is the world's only restaurant visited by both outlaw Jesse James and Brooke Shields, according to its owner.)

The menu features Midwest classics such as chicken and mashed potatoes, Mississippi River catfish, salad and vegetables from the family's organic garden, and memorable pies (leave room for the red raspberry or banana cream). Sundays, folks come for miles for the cinnamon rolls.

During fall foliage season, (when this area is at its most winsome) know that if you stop here on the weekend you'll be lucky to get a table; but other days it's so quiet you can hear an antique clock ticking nearby.

Bar with a View

The best part about Breitbach's may be in the bar, behind which is a cool mural of the spectacular view overlooking the Mississippi River valley nearby. The story goes that in 1934, a small band of gypsies straggled into Breitbach's Mercantile asking for food and lodging. With no money, they offered the artistic services of Alberto, their mural painter. He would paint a mural of the scenic landscape nearby! Which would someday be very valuable! In exchange, the Breitbachs would feed them and keep a roof over their heads! Whether the original proprietors believed this was a good deal or not, they agreed.

So, Alberto painted the mural, complete with biplane that flew overhead one day as he painted. His work netted the group $15 and a two-week stay before they moved on. Years passed, the room was remodeled with paneling, and the mural forgotten.

Then, a few years ago, the room was once again remodeled. The old 1954 paneling was peeled away, and, wonder of wonders! There was Alberto's picture on the wall, complete with biplane and Alberto's signature, just like he'd left it years before.

Dubuque

Café Manna Java
269 Main Street, Phone: (563) 588-3105

Georgia Wagner and her sister Michelle Mihalakis offer artisan breads, wood-fired pizzas, and sweet pastries at Café Manna Java in Dubuque.

Located in the Old Main district of Dubuque, this friendly, aromatic shop is warm with the scents of strong espresso, savory bread, wood-fired pizza, and sweet pastries.

Opened by sisters Michelle Mihalakis and Georgia Wagner, the two say that when they saw the building's interior of old brick walls, they knew that this was where they wanted their hometown dream of a coffeehouse/ bakery/café to be.

But make no mistake, these hometown women have worldly tastes. Artisanal breads in-clude olive rosemary, cranberry walnut, sesame semolina, and sunflower rye. Baguettes rival the best I've tasted anywhere. I overheard one discriminating little lady say in a thick accent: "This is the best hard roll I've tasted since Sveden."

The bread is made by hand by Georgia ("I must have studied 20 bread books over the years," she says) and a crew who continually monitor the quality. "This is slow food," says Michelle. And "every morning is fresh." Pastries involve a three-day process, says Georgia, explaining "Anything good takes time."

Many recipes such as the chocolate raspberry cake with French vanilla frosting and carrot cake with slivered almonds are family secrets. Order a slice or an entire cake. Mornings, you can't go wrong with a chocolate chip scone, a fabulous sticky bun, or a delicate apricot Danish. Afternoons, check out pecan bars, a wedge of cheesecake, or those great old-fashioned brownies known as "blondies."

Lunchtime, there are hot panini sandwiches, wood-fired pizzas, generous fresh salads, and hearty soups. The room is spacious, with plenty of tables, windows that let the sunshine in, and a coffee bar made from an old altar railing. "You always hear about these coffee bars," says Michelle, "but you know, I'd never see a bar when I'd go into them." When she found some old church furniture for sale, Michelle decided, "since Dubuque has more bars and churches than anywhere," to combine the concept for furnishing their cafe. It seems fitting too, after hearing about the old Greek man who once told Georgia that her bread "was manna from heaven."

Pepper Sprout
378 Main Street, Phone: (563) 556-2167

This chic bistro with exposed brick walls and tin ceiling serves everything from bison meatballs to pan-seared quail. Here, even the doggie bags look good; you know there's a chef who cares in the kitchen when your leftovers come out wrapped in foil that's been shaped into a swan.

The chef behind this oasis of culinary creativity in a land of meat and potatoes is local woman Kim Wolff. She, along with her father Clark, converted what was once a Chinese restaurant in Dubuque's Old Main district into a dining establishment that recognizes its history while putting a gourmet spin on the Midwest cuisine it promotes.

The long, narrow interior of the restored place features booths along one wall as well as leather-like tables graced with fresh miniature sunflowers. The menu is small, varies seasonally, and uses organic and locally grown produce. Homemade stocks, homemade breads, and wines chosen by Jamie Carroll from the nearby Grape Harbor add to its local appeal. But I'd have to say the pïëce de rèsistance the night I dined here was Wolff's preparation of pork. Arriving like a small roast, this succulent pork loin cut like butter and was served with just the right balance of sweetness—a few grilled strawberries and grapes, atop a savory blue cheese sauce, a winning combination.

Lunch and a Nap

Regarded as the world's shortest, steepest scenic railway, the Fenelon Place Elevator connects downtown Dubuque with a residential neighborhood on top of a steep bluff. It was erected in 1882 by businessman J. K. Graves, who worked downtown but liked to return home each afternoon for lunch and a nap. Unfortunately, in those days it took him a good hour to drive his horse and buggy home and back again. Remembering cable cars he'd seen on his trips to Europe, he decided to solve his lunch and nap problem by commissioning a similarly built cable car to be installed on the bluff near his home. It worked so well that it wasn't long before Graves's neighbors started asking permission to use the elevator too. Through the years it eventually became a city fixture. Today, it's listed on the National Register of Historic Places. Open April through November, the lift is 296 feet in length, and elevates passengers 189 feet from Fourth Street to Fenelon Place. From here, a magnificent view of Iowa, Illinois, and Wisconsin can be enjoyed. At the foot of the elevator, you'll find shops in the Cable Car Square shopping district.

Grape Harbor
123 Main Street, Phone (563) 582-6440

Whether you're a serious wine enthusiast or not, you won't want to miss Jamie Carroll's wine shop. Situated a stone's throw from the Mississippi River, it's another of the renovated buildings in Dubuque's Old Main district. With its hardwood floors and exposed brick interior, it seems a perfect fit for Jamie's worldly collection of wine.

But there's more than wine in this shop. In the front, a tiny deli case holds gourmet picnic fixings: wild smoked sockeye salmon, jars of caviar, wedges of French brie, and Josef Schmidt chocolates. In back of the shop, a small wine bar has chalkboards overhead listing the day's offerings. Another few steps puts you in an adjoining room loaded with wine accessories, gadgets, olive spoons, plastic picnic cocktail shakers with recipes printed on them, Reidel stemware, and even some artsy furniture. "We say we're a wine store that sells lamps," says Jamie with a laugh.

Clearly, this is not a shop designed for popping in and out of quickly. And while the gift items and picnic fare are enticing, it's the incredible selection of wines that keeps folks coming back. With over twenty years as a wine rep, Jamie knows her vino—and has thoughtfully chosen the wines that grace the walls here with knowledge and great care. Like most wine shop owners, she's passionate about wine, and loves to discuss, advise, and help customers select just the right bottle for any occasion.

Say you need a bottle of wine for a meal and you only want to spend twelve bucks? Jamie can select one. A baptism celebration? Jamie has one with a label of a baby's hand. "I once had a guy come in whose girlfriend broke up with him right before Valentine's Day, says Jamie, "and he wanted a bottle of wine to give her, so I showed him one labeled d'Arenberg's The Last Ditch."

She's got wines from $10 to $500, from hard-to-find small producers such as Jory— "40 cases of one Syrah is all they make," says Jamie—to Iron Horse— "it's served in the White House. Yes, there's a story behind all of them," she adds. Jamie also stocks many difficult-to-find wines produced in wineries that range from California to France, Argentina, and Chile. When the sommelier for Chicago's Spiaggia, one of the city's most well-respected eateries, stopped in and bought over $400 worth of wine, he told her, "There's nothing like this in Chicago."

"For a guy who's a real wine connoisseur," says Jamie, "this place is sort of like a room full of supermodels; they just don't know where to start."

A Food-Friendly Place to Stay

The Redstone Inn and Suites
504 Bluff Street
Phone: (563) 582-1894

Built in 1894 and located in the heart of downtown Dubuque, this Queen Anne mansion was constructed by Augustine A. Cooper, owner of Cooper Wagon Works. With its fairy-tale towers and turrets, stained glass, and Italian marble fireplaces, the Victorian home was actually a wedding gift for Cooper's daughter.

Today, the Redstone is a bed and breakfast with 15 rooms open for guests, and breakfast a casually civilized affair served at separate little tables in the elegant dining room.

Perhaps the nicest part about staying here, though, is having a chance to share a glass of wine with innkeeper Jerry Lazore in the opulent parlor—chatting about what to see and do in Dubuque, and, of course, where to eat and drink.

Lazore is a wealth of information, from where to watch eagles to where to find great prime rib (try Sweeney's Supper Club). Looking for an authentic Irish bar in town? Check out The Busted Lift, a pub with Irish entertainment to go with your Guinness. The club is in the basement of 180 Main Street, and on the first floor there really is a broken elevator, says Jerry.

Summer Saturday mornings, Lazore advises not to miss Dubuque's Farmers' Market. Especially look for the nuns' stand, where you can purchase homemade orange rolls and cinnamon bread.

Blueberry Muffins from the Redstone

This recipe is from Kelly Lazore, who prepares the muffins as part of the Redstone breakfast. They're quick, easy, and delicious. She buys her blueberries fresh at the Dubuque Farmers' Market.

1 1/2 cups flour

1/2 cup sugar

1 teaspoon baking powder

1 teaspoon salt

2 eggs, beaten

1/2 cup butter (use the real stuff, says Kelly Lazore)

1 cup milk

1 1/2 cups fresh blueberries

Whisk the dry ingredients together in a separate bowl. In another bowl, whisk the wet ingredients. Fold the dry and wet together, then add the blueberries.

Bake at 375 to 400 degrees for 25 minutes or until they pop back up when you press down.

Recipe courtesy of Kelly Lazore and reprinted with permission.

Czipar's Apple Orchard
8610 Route 52 South, Phone: (563) 582-7476

Located four miles south of Dubuque on Highway 52 is one of the prettiest orchards in the state. Czipar's Apple Orchard is set on the limestone bluffs high above the Mississippi River. Wander among the apple trees here and you can see parts of three states—Iowa, Illinois, and Wisconsin.

This family-oriented business has been in operation since 1938 when Joe Czipar planted a couple hundred apple trees on the little 10-acre plot here. A small lean-to shed served as his apple clearing house, and a one-bedroom house served as home. When Joe died in 1961, Joan and Dick Czipar (at the time recently married), purchased the property and began adding on to the house as well as improving the apple orchard.

Today, they raise 18 varieties of apples, including Royal Gala, Honeycrisp,

Czipar's Apple Orchard along Highway 52 just south of Dubuque.

Jonalicious, McIntosh, Cortland, and the Jon-a-red—a cross between a Red Delicious and a Jonathan apple, which Joan says is good for pie.

Apples are washed, sorted, graded, and packaged in three- and five-pound packages, then sold in the Apple House orchard store. Cheerfully bright with country red-and-white checked accents, the shop is loaded with lots more than apples. Don't be surprised if while you're shopping, Joan arrives from her home kitchen (across the lawn) carrying warm apple pies just out of the oven to sell at the store. Apple bread is also for sale here, and it hardly seems right to leave without buying one of each. (In fact, the day I was here two guys were purchasing pies for a political benefit in Dubuque while a woman from Chicago was loading up a pie to take home. "You've never tasted a pie like this," she informed me.)

Czipar's is also known for its homemade apple cider. This is pure apple juice, fully inspected. It's hard to buy good cider because most is pasteurized, says Joan. Czipar's is not. They sell it in half-gallon and one-gallon sizes, and it freezes beautifully, according to Joan. That is, of course, if you don't drink it all up immediately.

Betty Jane Caramel Apples are another treat that's hard to resist here. These come from the Home of the Gremlins—a Dubuque candy store—and use the Czipar's Jon-a-red apple as their base.

Inside the orchard store, you'll also find jars of apple and pumpkin butter, local elderberry and maple syrup, and Mason jars stuffed with hand-picked black walnuts, along with recipes for pumpkin bread and black walnut pie.

In late September, Czipar's annual Apple Festival takes place, drawing thousands of people. Besides a flea market, there are children's events, face painting, and plenty of entertainment. There are apples and kettle corn to munch on; even the local church pitches in and serves up roast pork barbeque sandwiches with all the trimmings.

Two Recipes from Czipar's

These two recipes from Czipar's Orchard are "Made Especially Good When Using Flo's Hand-Picked Iowa Black Walnuts!" You'll find jars stuffed with these black walnuts available for sale at the shop.

Melt-in-Your-Mouth-Pumpkin Bread

$1^1/4$ cups cooking oil

2 cups pumpkin

2 cups flour

$3/4$ cup black walnuts, chopped

2 3-ounce boxes coconut pie filling (not instant)

4 eggs

1 teaspoon salt

1 teaspoon baking soda

Mix oil, eggs, and pumpkin. Combine remaining ingredients and add to pumpkin mixture. Divide the mixture in two 9x5x3-inch greased loaf pans. Bake at 325 degrees for approximately 1 hour or until toothpick stuck in comes out clean.

Black Walnut Pie

3 eggs, lightly beaten

1 tablespoon lemon juice

1 cup light corn syrup

1 teaspoon vanilla

1 cup dark brown sugar

$2^1/2$ cups black walnuts

$1/4$ cup butter, melted

9-inch piecrust

Preheat oven to 350 degrees. Check the pie crust to be sure the edges are at least $1/4$ to $1/2$ inch above the rim of the pan to prevent the pie filling from bubbling over the edge. Gently combine all ingredients, in order listed. Stir enough to begin dissolving the sugar, but not enough to incorporate air into the filling. Do not beat or the pie will have air bubbles on the top instead of black walnuts, spoiling the glossy look of the glazed nuts.

Pour the mixture into the unbaked piecrust. Place on a cookie sheet and bake for one hour, or until the center of the pie is no longer loose and the black walnuts are browned. Serve either hot or cold, but for the best appearance allow the pie to reach room temperature before cutting. Whipped cream or ice cream makes a wonderful addition.

Courtesy of Czipar's Orchard and reprinted with permission.

Our Lady of the Mississippi Abbey
8400 Abbey Hill, Phone: (563) 582-2595; (563) 556-6330 for candy

Tucked into the rolling bluffs overlooking the Mississippi River south of Dubuque, this tranquil, tree-filled setting supplies spiritual nourishment to 21 Trappistine nuns of the Order of the Cistercians of the Strict Observance. It also supplies caramel lovers some of the best buttery treats they're likely to find anywhere in the state. The nuns sell their Trappistine Creamy Caramels by mail and through their Web site, but if you're driving the Great River Road, a visit here makes a lovely stop.

Driving south on Highway 52, it's easy to miss the turn-off for the abbey. Best bet is to keep track of the miles (about 5 1/2) out of Dubuque and keep a lookout for the small sign for the abbey. There is a gravel road to the east, and soon you'll see another sign and the stone-flanked

In the fall, be sure to stop at Our Lady of the Mississippi Abbey south of Dubuque for homemade caramels.

drive into the grounds. Follow the road in, and watch for the gift shop. The candy kitchen itself is not open to the public.

Inside the gift/candy shop, it's serenely sensual with the aroma of chocolate, cream, and butter infusing the small office-like room. Besides the cellophane-wrapped vanilla and chocolate caramels, there are also caramels dipped in chocolate, smooth, chocolatey rich Irish and Swiss mints, and milk chocolate hazelnut meltaways. Bowls are filled with bits of sweet samples. Don't be shy. Taste. Besides small bags of the caramels, you can buy the caramels in bulk: five-pound boxes contain approximately 240 pieces. Beautiful embossed gift boxes feature various assortments of the other offerings.

At Mississippi Abbey, "candy season" is from September through December, and has been in operation since 1965. Following the rule of St. Benedict that their living should be made by the labor of their hands, that was the year when 13 Trappistine nuns here cooked their first batch of caramel, using a time-honored recipe from the motherhouse in Wrentham, Massachusetts. In 1973, the nuns began hand-dipping some of their vanilla caramels in fine milk chocolate. As production increased, they eventually purchased a chocolate-coating machine. In the 1980s, Irish mints and Swiss mints were added to the nuns' repertoire of the sweet stuff. Today, 21 sisters cook and process over 60,000 pounds of caramel and 10,000 pounds of mints in preparation for Christmas orders.

Best of all, when you purchase these wondrous beauties, you're doubly blessed. Why? According to the nuns' caramel catalog: "Your support of the products enables us to be faithful to our contemplative life of prayer, manual labor, and spiritual reading. We in turn promise to hold you in our prayers throughout the day." How many other boxes of candy can offer such a guarantee?

Bellevue

Riverview Hotel and Restaurant
100 South Riverview, Phone: (563) 872-4142

You can't go wrong with breakfast (hash browns and eggs), lunch (a smoked turkey BLT, homespun grilled cheese) or dinner (Cajun-spiked pork) any day at the Riverview. But if you're looking for fresh-from-scratch pie, this is the place you want to be on a Thursday or Friday, preferably around noon, when the fresh pies come out of the oven. Thursdays it's the meringue pies, and Fridays it's the cream pies.

Located on Bellevue's lengthy Main Street that parallels the Mississippi and the town's Riverfront Park, the Riverview has been around for years. This is the kind of hometown café where the waitresses say stuff like, "Okay, honey, how you want that done?" and groups of local retired business guys gather in the morning for coffee. Booths and tables fill the sunny corner space and windows offer views of the river across the street.

If you're looking for a cheap room for the night (and you've called ahead— necessary on autumn weekends), you can pick up the key from the restaurant/bar/hotel/owner, and simply walk upstairs. The rooms are small, the floors tilt a bit, but they're clean and come complete with a small rocking chair and a little balcony that allows you to sit and look out at the river. (Free morning cups of coffee from the restaurant are part of the deal.)

Clinton

Rastrelli's Restaurant
238 Main Avenue, Phone: (563) 242-7441

Rastrelli's was recommended to me at the hotel I stayed at the first time I visited Clinton.

This Italian favorite is in the old part of Clinton, across the street from the Sweetheart Bakery. It's one of those old family restaurants where the menu is interspersed with blurry but beloved black-and-white photos of the Mom and Pop who obviously started the place—plus snapshots of the family, long ago waitresses, and the original soda fountain that was once part of the business.

Today's Rastrelli's (it moved to its current location in 1950) is a hodgepodge of rooms, some with framed photographs of the family on the walls, another area boasting a pretty Italian mural. There are green cushy booths, windows out to the street, the requisite salad bar the first thing you see when you walk in, and friendly, helpful servers. This is a family dining room the way it used to be.

The menu includes Italian standbys such as manicotti with Rastrelli's meatless tomato sauce, ravioli, tortellini, and lasagna—and all entrees include unlimited trips to the salad bar.

The Italian pasta dishes are all good, but the truth is most people come here for the irresistible pizza. The story goes that when current owner Mike Rastrelli's brother Bob came home from the Navy in the 1950s, he brought with him the idea of selling pizza at his dad Pete's restaurant. A sister, Carol, who had been living in Chicago around the same time, also had the idea—as did Mike's Chicago godfather. With the candy business declining and his family pushing the pizza concept, Pete decided to try the then-innovative dish—and in 1955, Pete and Ida introduced their special recipe of pizza to Clinton. Since that time, it has built a loyal following.

For dessert, there's the standard tiramisu or spumoni, but Pete's Original Hot Fudge Sundae, which comes with its own little pitcher of the hot home-made goo on the side, is the way to go.

A Little Rastrelli History

In 1939, Pete and Ida Rastrelli opened Rastrelli's Revere Candy Shop in the Revere Hotel at Fourth Avenue South and Second Street. The Revere had a long soda fountain with a marble and stainless steel back bar, 50 mahogany booths, a popcorn machine, glass cigar cases, and soda jerks in white shirts and bow ties. The Revere was a very popular place to meet and hang out. Many couples shared their first date here over a Revere sundae. The menu featured burgers, sandwiches, and also Dad's handmade ice cream and candies. Does anyone remember the Olive Nut Sandwich?

-from the restaurant menu

Courtesy of Mike Rastrelli and reprinted with permission

Quad Cities

Whitey's Ice Cream
Numerous locations, Phone: (888) 5WHITEY

Everybody loves Whitey's—a Quad Cities tradition since 1933—and why wouldn't they? This cheery red-and-white striped place is all about some of the best ice cream anywhere. Creamy and rich, it's in dozens of different flavors: vanilla, chocolate, cherry, black raspberry, fresh peach, fresh banana, lime, root beer, and blueberry to name a few.

And no matter which store you choose to visit (there are currently a dozen locations), expect a crowd. There's always a line, especially on hot summer nights when people are cooling off with cones and sundaes, sodas and shakes—and something absolutely amazing called a Boston. This diet-busting, heart-stopping number is basically a malt or shake of your choice (I'll take a Kona coffee ice cream shake) topped with a sundae of your choice (I'll take a couple scoops of the Kona coffee ice smothered in Whitey's hot fudge). Can you say *decadent*? You can choose all sorts of creative combinations with a Boston if you're so inclined. The strangest one I've heard to date is an orange sherbet and Kit Kat shake, topped with a black raspberry sundae with Butterfinger. I think I got that straight. "It's the most unusual one I made this week," the girl scooping out my ice cream informed me.

Whitey's began in 1935 as a little ice cream shop in Moline, Illinois. Owned by Chester "Whitey" Lindgren, Whitey hired 15-year-old Bob Tunberg to help out in the store. In 1953, Bob and his wife Norma purchased the shop from his mentor and friend. Today, sons Jon and Jeff work side by side as the company's co-owners. The title of President remains open in honor of their father Bob, the "Quad-Cities' Favorite Ice Cream Man," who passed away in 1991.

Whitey's Old-Fashioned Fudge Sauce

1 cup heavy whipping cream

1 3/4 cups butter, cubed

1 1/3 cups packed brown sugar

1/3 cup sugar

Pinch salt

1 cup baking cocoa

1/2 cup plus 2 tablespoons light corn syrup

2 squares (1 ounce each) unsweetened chocolate

3 teaspoons vanilla extract

1 to 2 teaspoons rum extract

1. In a heavy saucepan, combine cream and butter. Cook and stir over medium-low heat until butter is melted. Add the sugars and salt; cook and stir until sugar is dissolved, about 4 minutes. Stir in the cocoa and corn syrup; cook and stir for 3 minutes or until cocoa is blended.

2. Add chocolate; cook and stir 3 to 4 minutes longer or until chocolate is melted. Reduce heat to low. Simmer for 12 to16 minutes or until desired thickness is reached, stirring constantly. Remove from the heat; stir in extracts. Cool slightly. Serve warm over ice cream. Refrigerate leftovers.

Yield: about 3 1/2 cups.
Recipe courtesy of Whitey's Ice Cream and reprinted with permission.

Bettendorf

Ross' Restaurant
430 14th Street, Phone: (563) 355-7573

Located partially under a freeway overpass and at the bottom of a hill (down from The Abbey Hotel), it seems sort of ironic that this nondescript place is known as the home of the Magic Mountain.

For the uninitiated, a Magic Mountain (created by Ron Freidhof, who owns the place with his wife Cynthia Ross Freidhof) starts out with grilled Texas toast. Then it's topped with hash browns (you can get French fries, but for an extra quarter, opt for the hash browns) before being loaded with Ross's loose-meat. Finally, the whole concoction gets smothered with cheese sauce. That's unless you want your Mountain also "capped with snow." Then the grand finale is a bunch of chopped raw onions sprinkled on top. The Mountain also comes in variations including the Volcano. This hot and spicy version gets topped with Ross's famously delicious chili. Is this road food at its finest, or what?

Opened in its hard-to-get-to location in 1965, Ross's color scheme matches the era—turquoise booths match the turquoise counter stools. Glass partitions between booths are etched with the outline of a mountain and the words "Home of the Magic Mountain" printed inside. Waitresses have been here forever. The place is sparkling clean. Family recipes fill the menu, along with quotes about (and pictures of) the late Harold Ross, who opened his first restaurant in 1938 in Toledo, Iowa. He was obviously a beloved man. Notorious for making double-or-nothing wagers with customers, usually he won—unless the customer was down on his luck. Then the customer always walked away a winner. He was also notorious with the regular 10 a.m. coffee-break crowd, whom he would entertain with what locals called "half-sermon, half-lecture, and half-comedy routine." Fuzzy black-and-white photos in the menu show Harold in a hula skirt, and another with his beloved bowling ball, which he apparently had dubbed "Elvis." You just don't get these kinds of stories (or food) when you stop at a Perkins for pancakes by the freeway.

Today, Harold's daughter Cynthia and her husband own and run the restaurant. Breakfast is served round the clock, and just about everything you order here is going to be down-home good. The place is hard to find, but with its personality and history, it's well worth searching out.

A Food-Friendly Place to Stay

The Abbey Hotel
1401 Central Avenue
Phone: (563) 355-0291; (800) 438-7535

From the exterior, with its angelic statues and stained glass windows, it's not hard to believe this magnificent Romanesque structure, high atop a bluff in Bettendorf, was for many years a cloistered Carmelite monastery. But the interior nowadays hardly bespeaks the austere conditions the Sisters once lived in.

Totally transformed into an elegant bed and breakfast (truly one of the most unusual in the country), the lobby today features

The Abbey Hotel in Bettendorf is one of the most elegant and unusual bed and breakfasts in the country.

Italian marble (as do the gorgeous bathrooms). You'll also find crystal chandeliers and 19 guest rooms: as many as five of the original cells have been put together to make one beautiful room. However, the doors to the original nuns' rooms have been preserved on the hallway side to maintain the monastery appearance. There's also a museum "room" on the third floor, furnished and maintained in its original size and configuration, that shows the way a Carmelite Sister once lived her life in the monastery.

Nowadays, pleasing tones of peaches, mauves, and blues accent luxurious silken draperies in the rooms, and sitting areas in some of the oversized rooms (along with the most beautiful, comfortable beds you'll ever sleep in) make this hotel room one you won't be in a rush to leave, even to eat. In fact, what's super about staying here is that you don't have to. You can order off an elegant little menu and have your dinner brought to your room. Or if you like, go get yourself a pizza at Harris Pizza (they've been a Quad Cities favorite for decades) and bring it back to the inn.

In the morning, a breakfast is served in the sunroom (which really isn't all that sunny) on the main floor. But if you're smart, you take your fine, fresh repast up to the second floor verandah, where tables are set up and you can look out the stone arches, over the apple trees and manicured grounds to the Mississippi River in the distance. There you can sip your coffee, tuck into your quiche, enjoy your pastry, and count your blessings.

Davenport

Boozies Bar and Grill
114 ½ West Third Street, Phone: (563) 328-2929

A bar called Boozies may sound exactly like what it is. But it's not. Well, it's a bar all right, and a local favorite to be sure, in a building that dates to 1899 in downtown Davenport (see sidebar for more information on its location). But Boozie is the name of a cat. And this establishment's claim to fame (besides its awesome burgers) is that this was the first downtown business owned and operated by a feline. It's true. Boozie's portrait hangs on the wall here. Nearby, there's also a plaque that states: "Sadly, Boozie is no longer with us. But we continue on his tradition of catering to our clientele with good food served by good people. Boozie would have wanted it that way."

The thing to order here is a Boozie Burger: a third of a pound of exceptional Iowa ground beef, piled high with three cheeses, bacon, lettuce, tomato, onion, pickles, mayo, and some kickin' Boozie sauce. If you want your burger "flaming" you'll get Boozie's hot wing sauce and hot pepper cheese with it instead.

Spiritual Nourishment for Body and Mind

Besides Boozie's interesting feline history, perhaps even more—dare we say—unusual, is the location of Boozies bar itself. See, if you walk up the half staircase (it's situated like an old New York City brownstone), there's Boozies. But if you walk down the half staircase to the garden-level shop directly underneath Boozies—well, you'll be in The Faith Explained bookshop (Catholic books and gifts).

Mac's Tavern
316 West Third Street, Phone: (563) 324-6227

If you are lucky enough to be in Davenport when the Bix Beiderbecke Jazz Festival takes place (late July), take the opportunity to stop in this historic tavern. The curved bar seems to stretch for a mile, there are dark wood booths along the wall, and an old tiled floor. Framed posters from previous Bix Festivals line the walls and there's even a trombone over the bar itself. The place is spotlessly clean, and one of the women bartenders (here since 1975) is straight out of Cheers. She's the one who'll inform you that this place has a "Heinz 57" variety of people, and not only has she "seen it all" in her years here, sometimes she's seen more than she wanted to see.

If owner Bill Collins is around, and he usually is (unless the cook locked his keys in the car and Bill has to go back in the kitchen and play chef), he's got great stories to share (the bar has an interesting history). "I was on my way to a meeting 15 years ago, walked in here when I saw it was for sale, and never left," he says.

The old Irish bar—it opened in September 1934—has seen its share of celebs: Tanya Tucker and Peggy Lee, just to name two. Not to mention the local powers that be—lawyers and bankers, judges and CEOs. It's another of the beloved local hangouts, with loyal clientele. The sign outside boasts "Fine Food," and it is.

During the Bix Festival, a band sets up in the street, right outside its door. The music and people (thousands) turn the entire area into one big party. It's a great time to visit. Then again, Mac's is the kind of place you don't really need a reason to stop in.

A sign of the times along the Great River Road.

Exotic Thai
2303 East 53rd Street, Phone: (563) 344-0909

In a strip mall, next to a dry-cleaning establishment, this unassuming little spot feels sophisticated and serene, even though it's often packed with people (do make reservations on the weekend) and décor is minimal.

"Experience Faraway Flavors" says the menu, and indeed, with these offerings you can. The lengthy list is broken down into several categories: Rice is Nice, Long Life Noodles, Madam Curry, Sensuous Seafood, Adventures—all with detailed descriptions so you know exactly what you're getting.

You certainly can't go wrong with their pad thai, but don't be afraid to try their spicy basil noodles—a well-seasoned blend of chilies and basil, flat rice noodles, and pepper. Ditto a Dancing Shrimp Salad—grilled shrimp sparkling atop greens. Be forewarned, these last two are not for those whose idea of spicy is Taco Bell's hot sauce. These dishes are spiced Thai style—fiery but not so much that it kills your taste buds.

Complimentary tea is served upon request. Afterward, you need only drive down the street a couple blocks and you can cool off your palate with some of Whitey's ice cream for dessert.

Sherry Freese's Baker's Dozen Iowa Food Favorites

Sherry K. Freese is the regional editor of *Home & Away* magazine for AAA Minnesota/Iowa.

Whitey's Ice Cream, Bettendorf. Turtle Sundae

Jaarsma Bakery, Pella. Dutch Letters (and anything else in the case!)

David's Diner, Perry (Hotel Pattee). Anything the chef prepares

Happy Joe's Pizza (throughout the state). Canadian bacon/sauerkraut pizza

Danish Inn, Elk Horn. Thursday night crab legs buffet

Machine Shed (Davenport, West Des Moines). Iowa pork chops and apple dumpling

Waterfront Deli, Bettendorf. Cardiac sandwich

Café Express, Davenport. Homemade curried chicken sandwich on wheat bread

Ox Yoke Restaurant, Amana. Family-style fried chicken, cottage cheese with chives, sauerkraut, and rhubarb pie

Sneaky Pete's, LeClaire. Cowboy beans and baked potato

Faithful Pilot, LeClaire. Crab cakes

Filling Station, Davenport. Pork tenderloin sandwich with a bun as big as the tenderloin

Breitbach's, Balltown. Homemade soups and Cindy's pies

Southeast Region
American Gothic, Rhubarb Pie, and Biscuits

Meandering along a country road in Southeast Iowa at twilight, there comes a point where the line between past and present becomes blurred—and time elusive. Driving by small-town baseball fields and well-kept barns, or church steeples gracefully etched against a backdrop of clouds turning pink, one can almost forget this is the twenty-first century. This is truly rural life at its most slow-paced and serene—intermingled with a sense of history and timelessness that always seems to pervade such quietness.

This is a region where villages don't need stoplights, where you're more likely to smell supper cooking at home than see a fast-food franchise, and where—should you find a place to eat—it's a good bet you'll find pie on the menu, probably made with rhubarb from somebody's garden.

It's also a region rich in rural charms and proud of tradition, even if it means fighting with the city officials occasionally to keep something as simple as Ottumwa's Canteen in the Alley, a small eat shack established in the 1920s that has a cement parking ramp literally built around it.

Artists are drawn to the area, and while the Agency Gallery Deli seems an unlikely place for an art gallery, there it is, with artists' works changing monthly on the walls in this spotlessly clean dining room. In truth, the area has been popular with artists for decades. Consider that Grant Wood drove through this country for inspiration years ago; in sleepy Eldon you can follow the signs to see the house he sketched on an envelope that would eventually become part of his most famous painting.

Farther south, the villages of Van Buren County continue the aura of a region that time seems to have forgotten (or at least allowed to tick at a less frenzied speed).

The first little Van Buren burg, Keosauqua, is a demure treasure of a village. Named after an Indian word meaning "great bend" (in reference to the loop the Des Moines River takes around it), quiet Keosauqua wasn't always thus. For years, the town noisily thrived as one of the ports along this once-bustling passageway for steamboats. The village was also a fording spot for the Mormons on their westward trek in the late 1840s as well as a stop on the Underground Railroad.

These days Keosauqua's small downtown depends on tourism more than anything. Consisting of eating places such as the Riverbend Pizza and Steakhouse or George's Pizza and Steakhouse (the two next-door neighbors have a friendly competition going), it also boasts the Village Cup and Cakes. This is a great place to purchase picnic provisions (e.g., iced lattes, well-made sandwiches, layer cake) to pack in a basket and take out to nearby Lacey-Keosauqua State Park for a meal with a view.

To the west of town is Lebanon, home to several Amish and Mennonite families; drop down a few miles farther and consider a detour over to Cantril, where a stop at the Dutchman's Store will net you spices, noodles, boxes of funnel cake mix, and even bolts of fabric.

Bentonsport is another quiet beauty, with antique and craft shops lining the riverfront. Walk along the 1882 one-lane iron bridge over the Des Moines River for shoreline vistas and Kodak moments.

In Bonaparte, the entire downtown area is considered a National Historic District. One of the most popular stops here is at Bonaparte's Retreat, a restaurant housed in a nineteenth-century gristmill, where you'll be served some of the best food in the region.

From Van Buren County it's not far to Keokuk, a city that lies at the most southeasterly tip of the state. At the confluence of the Des Moines River and Mississippi River, Keokuk's location played a key part during the Civil War, when seven hospitals were established here to care for the wounded transported up the Mississippi River from southern battlefields. Others may recognize Keokuk's name for a more literary reason: yes, this is the town where Mark Twain worked as a young man in the printing shop of his brother Orion

Grant Wood's American Gothic has been parodied in all sorts of ways, even by residents of his home state. In Eldon, you can see the house that became part of one of the most famous paintings of all time.

170

Clemens. If you're hungry, head down near the river and check out The Cellar—famous for their hamburgers (they're known for marvelous half pounders) and fresh-from-the-fry-kettle onion rings.

North from Keokuk lies Fort Madison, one of my favorite river towns as well as the first place I learned about one of Iowa's unusual culinary traditions—caramel sticky rolls in the dinner bread basket. Fort Madison is also where I first experienced and tasted fried strawberries. Chef Kumar Wickramasingha whips ups these lightly aromatic, sweetly warm treats at Alpha's on the Riverfront. Since 1994, the personable Kumar (from Sri Lanka) has been introducing Fort Madison's natives to all sorts of innovative tastes—and winning awards (and fans) in the process.

The river town also boasts a large Hispanic population. Besides its Mexican Fiesta in September, it's an easy place to find authentic tacos and enchiladas—try Vel's Amigos (choose from its train caboose take-out location or its sit-down restaurant with a liquor license) or El Zarapes Supper Club.

Burlington is another historic southeast Mississippi River town, and a stop at the Port of Burlington (which houses an Iowa Welcome Center) offers a great view of the stunning Great River Bridge, an elegantly graceful $60 million cable-stayed bridge spanning Twain's ever-majestic and always-changing Mississippi River.

Burlington's Snake Alley

Once dubbed by *Ripley's Believe It or Not* as the "crookedest street in the world," Snake Alley was constructed in 1894, and originally built as an experimental street connecting the downtown business district with the neighborhood shopping area on North Sixth Street. Constructed of tilted bricks (designed to allow better footing for horses), the 275-foot-long street zigzags nearly 60 feet up the bluff. Unfortunately, the switchback design was not as successful as anticipated—it seems drivers still lost control of their horses on such steep curves—and plans to copy the model were abandoned.

Ottumwa

Canteen in the Alley
112 East Second Street, Phone: (641) 682-5320

It's not easy to find, but ask anyone in town and they'll know what you're talking about when you mention the "Canteen"—the little eat shack with a parking ramp literally built over and around it.

Established by "Dusty" Rhoades in 1927, according to the framed history of the diner here, the Canteen in the Alley was originally located 30 feet east of its present building and seated five people. In 1936, it moved to today's site, and has been serving up its famous loosemeat sandwich (the Canteen), along with malts, pop, pie, and ice cream ever since.

The place is still small, just like its menu, but now it has at least 10 red cushioned stools surrounding a horseshoe-shaped counter. This allows customers to watch the aproned cook in the middle stirring and frying up the loosemeat that goes in your sandwich. The grill is slanted, allowing the grease to drain off on its own, and it's deep, so that a lot of beef can be stirred up at the same time. If you order your Canteen with everything, you get a thick swipe of cheese, a pile of pickles, and squirt of catsup loaded on, plus a generous sprinkling of salt. But regulars all have their preferences. Lunchtime, it's not uncommon to hear: "A canteen to go, with everything but the pickles, easy on the salt."

After you've ordered your Canteen and the meat has been loaded into the bun, it's loosely wrapped up in a waxed paper square and served to you with a spoon (to spoon up all the loosemeat that invariably falls out of it).

The walls at the eatery (the place was saved from demolition by a woman who fought tirelessly to keep it from being torn down) contain faded framed photos of John F. Kennedy and Franklin Roosevelt. Old wooden glass display shelves hold the array of pies that are listed on the back wall: raisin, strawberry rhubarb, apple, cherry, and more. Later in the afternoon, you can see the names of the day's sold-out ones covered over by masking tape. Know that you can order a half slice of pie if you're too full for a whole one. But do leave room, because warmed and served with a generous plop of ice cream, it's a real comfort-food treat.

Some Canteen Prices Through The Years

- 1929 Canteen Sandwich: Ten cents
- Pie, small: Five cents
- Pie, large: Ten cents
- Pop, in bottles: Five cents
- Sandwich, pop, and pie: Twenty-five cents
- 1942 Canteen Sandwich: Twenty-five cents
- 1976 Canteen Sandwich: Sixty cents
- 1994 Canteen Sandwich: $1.90
- 2004 Canteen Sandwich: $2.65

Agency

Agency Gallery Deli
115 West Main Street, Phone: (641) 937-5555

After the speed limit sign requires you to slow down here, start looking for the hanging flowerpots outside a small, rustic-sided storefront. When you see the bright blooms, see if the neon light in the window is shining "OPEN." If it is, consider yourself lucky. Next door to a uniform shop and one door down from Mrs. Bonser's egg noodle factory, this little dining room with a shoebox-sized kitchen is also an art gallery.

The steak sandwich is the specialty here, but I prefer their sweet and savory Monte Christo sandwich. Stacked with ham and cheese, it's grilled to buttery perfection, then dusted with powdered sugar, and served with strawberry preserves for dipping it in. When they say they make everything here—and that it's "fresh and lively"—believe them. Sandwiches are served with your choice of salad: potato, pasta, or Jell-O. When was the last time you were offered Jell-O as a salad option?

You can't leave without a piece of pie (especially because the display case is the first thing you see when you walk in here). Select from chocolate, pecan, cherry, or rhubarb. If you're a rhubarb aficionado, check out the 9x12 pan of icebox rhubarb dessert too.

A Food-Friendly Place To Stay

The Mansion Inn Bed & Breakfast
500 Henry Street, Keosauqua
Phone: (800) 646-0166; (319) 293- 2511

Driving up to the Mansion Inn Bed and Breakfast in Keosauqua feels a little like you're entering a southern-themed movie. Step inside this tall, elegant 1880s white-pillared mansion, and the antebellum aura continues. In the foyer, a gorgeous curved staircase sweeps upstairs past two stained glass windows. Take a peek in the parlor (nearly thirty feet long) and you can see specks of bright garden blooms through ten-foot windows that flank the fireplace and overlook the side lawn.

No, there aren't mint juleps waiting, but innkeepers William and Karen Sauter offer something even better on a hot Iowa afternoon—icy, fresh margaritas. Sit on the screened porch and sip one, and you realize what simple happiness and country living is all about. From here you can see Karen's gardens and birds galore. Stick around till twilight, and you'll be rewarded with the magic of fireflies—tiny dots of light that make the lawn seem to sparkle.

Both Karen and William grew up in the area, and their inn is a labor of love. This is not an overloaded lace and doily mansion filled with bric-a-brac. This is a big sprawling place where guys don't need to worry about feeling like a bull in a china shop. There's space to roam, whether you're upstairs on the verandah, downstairs in the dining room, watching television in the parlor (if you must, there's even a remote), or out on the grounds admiring the gardens.

In the morning, a full breakfast includes eggs and bacon, juice and fruit, and one of Karen's breakfast desserts—maybe a sweet strawberry Napoleon or a warm almond pastry stick. Served in the massive dining room, there are several tables if you prefer dining as a twosome. If you choose, take your coffee, sit out on the front porch, or meander through the house admiring the impressive collection of P. Buckley Moss prints.

Karen's Sauter's Margarita Mix

Keep a pitcher of this in your refrigerator, and you'll always be ready for guests.

1 12-ounce can limeade (frozen concentrate)

$1/3$ can triple sec

1 can tequila

3 cans cold water

Shake well. Keep in refrigerator.
To serve, shake mixture, pour over ice in glasses.
If you want to make a smaller batch, use a 6-ounce can of limeade and adjust proportions accordingly.
Recipe courtesy of Karen Sauter and reprinted with permission.

Bonaparte

Bonaparte's Retreat
813 Front Street, Phone: (800) 359-2590; (319) 592-3339

Drive into tiny Bonaparte on an autumn weekend, see the lines of people crowded down the steps from this restored 1878 gristmill, and you'll know you're at the right place for a meal.

Located on the Des Moines River (in back of the mill, there's a little terrace overlooking the water), the popular spot was designated a National Historic Site in 1983.

Inside, the rustic décor matches the building's history: original brick walls, two-foot-thick wood beams, a beautiful walnut-back bar, and a mix of collectibles that includes antique quilts and more. Locals fill many of the tables, but a quick glance at the guest book shows folks from all over the world have been sitting down at these tables to indulge.

At lunchtime, check out the chalkboard with the blue plate special noted, and order it—especially if it's the creamed chicken over heavenly biscuits. Other hearty country fare includes barbeque beef, meatballs, or a steaming hot breaded crisp of catfish on warm bread. Come dinnertime, the specialty is the rib eye steak. But don't be afraid to give the home-style canned beef a shot (it's different, but delicious!).

Rose Hendricks is the force within the kitchen here (and the biscuit maker)—and everybody knows she's the one who makes these simple Midwestern favorites shine. Save room for a slice of banana cream pie, and you're good to go.

Bonaparte's Landmark Mill

William Meek arrived in 1836 and established this mill, and within several years other flour, grist, and lumber mills lined the river, all powered by huge water wheels on the Des Moines. Settlers came to Bonaparte from as far as 100 miles away to have their grain ground into flour, and Meek's Mills and other mills established a reputation for quality.

Wagons loaded with grain and pulled by packhorses waited their turn to cross the wide Des Moines River on Meek's Ferry. Some customers waited in line for days to have their flour processed, and with their business, Bonaparte's hotels, taverns, and trading posts flourished.

Steamboats and paddle wheelers chugged up the river on their way to Des Moines, and the first Utah-bound Mormon settlers stopped in Bonaparte long enough to have their grist processed and to build several sturdy downtown buildings.

The machine age has long since taken its toll on the little village, but the spirit and atmosphere of the past pervade the old mill as Bonaparte's Retreat yet today.

Reprinted with permission from Bonaparte's Retreat bill of fare.

175

A Taste of Chocolate

Mid-September is when the Bonaparte Historical Society puts on its annual Chocolate Tasting Festival—and all things chocolate are put out for purchase at the bake sale.

If you miss the sweet-selling event, console yourself by making one of the recipes from their three-dollar recipe booklet. It includes many of the chocolate delights that have been sold through the years (for example, Raspberry Truffle Brownies, Caramel Fudge Cheesecake, Chocolate Mocha Cookies). Here's a favorite.

Buttermilk Chocolate Bread

$^1/_2$ cup butter

2 eggs

$^1/_2$ cup cocoa, unsweetened

$^1/_2$ teaspoon baking powder

1 cup buttermilk

1 cup sugar

1$^1/_2$ cups flour

$^1/_2$ teaspoon salt

$^1/_2$ teaspoon baking soda

$^1/_3$ cup chopped pecans

In a mixing bowl, cream butter and sugar. Add eggs, one at a time, beating well after each addition. Combine the flour, cocoa, salt, baking powder, and baking soda; add to creamed mixture alternately with buttermilk. Fold in pecans.

Pour into greased 9x5x3-inch loaf pan. Bake at 350 degrees for 45 to 50 minutes, or until a toothpick inserted near the center comes out clean. Cool for 10 minutes before removing from pan to a wire rack.

In a small mixing bowl, beat $^1/_2$ cup butter ("no substitutes") until fluffy. Add 2 tablespoons honey and 2 tablespoons chocolate syrup; mix well. Serve with bread.

Courtesy of the Bonaparte Historical Society and reprinted with permission.

Cantril

The Dutchman's Store
103 Division Street, Phone: (319) 397-2322

From aprons to harmonicas to suspenders and candy, this store (operated by a local Mennonite family) is reminiscent of an old-fashioned mercantile shop. An eclectic array of just about everything you could possibly need (or not) is stocked in this crammed-to-the-rafters emporium.

You'll find jars of pickled eggs next to jars of Ragu spaghetti sauce. There are bulk spices, cocoa mixes, itsy bitsy marshmallows, fabric, thread, crackers, cookies, and bread.

Out front on the boardwalk, there's often one of the local Amish families selling pans of cinnamon rolls and pies (peach and blueberry). If you're here in the autumn during the Forest Craft and Scenic Drive, the tiny main street of Cantril (population 250) is lively with people and filled with music. Do check out the local garage where songs such as "She Only Likes her Beer with Ice" are being performed with gusto.

Mount Sterling

AJ's Bar and Grill
101 Elm Street, Phone: (319) 494-5582

AJ's is a country tavern-type place in the midst of the rolling fields of Van Buren County. Rightly famous for their huge, fresh pork tenderloins, theirs are lightly hand-breaded and accompanied by corn nuggets (good little hush puppy-like morsels). Don't expect much ambiance here, though. The place is basically a big square building with a pool table in the middle and a bar to one side. Mounted deer heads on the wall proclaim that this is big hunting country. Although there are booths to sit in here, the best seats are at the bar, where huge windows look out on a serene panoramic vista of the countryside.

Fort Madison

Alpha's on the Riverfront
709 Avenue H (Highway 61), Phone: (319) 372-1411

At first glance, the menu at Alpha's seems a pretty traditional Midwestern compilation of the standard supper club fare: Caesar salad, grilled pork chops, barbequed ribs, filet mignon, shrimp, chicken breast, mashed potatoes.

But look a little closer and what's this? Curry flavored vegetable soup? Fried strawberries? Rosemary crusted breast of chicken over garlic and feta cheese potatoes? Bacon-wrapped green beans with roasted garlic bordelaise? This isn't the typical meat, mashed potato, green bean, and gravy entrees that Iowans are accustomed to.

Then again, this also isn't the typical restaurant chef that small towns in Iowa see everyday either. Alpha's chef/owner Kumar Wickramasingha is originally from Sri Lanka, and while he's been accommodating local palates since 1994 when he became Alpha's executive chef, he's also been oh-so-gradually infusing the menu's basic concepts with a dash of his homeland's flavors.

In the process, he managed to win several awards through the years—many in the Iowa Pork Producers Association's Taste of Elegance competition. In 2003, he was a National Pork Board Celebrated Chef.

Alpha's menu showcases a couple of his prize creations, and you are a fool if you don't order these winners. His fennel-infused pork loin and onion wraps arrive standing up—within a starburst circle of colorful brandy mustard and citrusy barbecue sauce. Not only are they a mini masterpiece, the mixture of flavors and scents sparkles deliciously.

Likewise, the marinated pork loin salad dazzles with a light freshness. It's served with soft and warm cheese bread, and the duo easily makes a delightful meal. Still, don't leave without tasting Kumar's "own perfect combination": rosemary crusted chicken breast with creamy garlic-and-feta mashed potatoes. There really is nothing nicer than digging into this gourmet pile of goodness while relaxing near the windows at Alpha's, with the Mississippi River moving lazily across the way.

When it's time for dessert, this is one place it should not be skipped. I was

Kumar's Kitchen Dreams

When Kumar Wickramasingha came to the United States (he had met friends here in Fort Madison while in a high school exchange program), he quickly discovered that his formal education and previous food-service experience as a banquet manager in Sri Lanka meant nothing outside of his home country. But his dream of having his own restaurant kept him going, and he worked his way up from dishwasher—eventually realizing his lifelong goal when he bought Alpha's on the Riverfront.

He has won numerous awards for innovative and tasty new ways with pork at the annual Iowa Pork Producers Association's Taste of Elegance competition. Here is one of his prize winners.

Alpha's Award Winning Marinated Pork Loin Salad

1 pound boneless pork loin

1 pound small mushrooms

$^1/_4$ sliced medium red onion

1 sliced small red bell pepper

1 sliced small yellow bell pepper

12 sun dried tomatoes

1 head Romaine lettuce

Salt and pepper to taste

Marinade

1 cup vegetable oil

$^1/_2$ cup balsamic vinegar

$^1/_4$ cup soy sauce

1 tablespoon fennel seeds

Season pork loin with salt and pepper. Bake until done, then cool. Thinly slice the pork loin and mix with the rest of the ingredients except the Romaine lettuce. Pour the marinade over and marinate overnight. Place torn Romaine lettuce over a plate. Arrange the marinated pork loin, mushrooms, tomatoes, and peppers over the lettuce.

Courtesy of Kumar Wickramasingha and reprinted with permission.

Tips on Ordering at Alpha's

The insert found within the menu for Alpha's on the Riverfront in Fort Madison contains this personal note from the chef.

Cooking food from my country Sri Lanka is very challenging because people in Iowa are not used to Southeastern spices, so I gave up on cooking Sri Lankan food for customers. For one of our Christmas banquets, I fixed a soup from my homeland and I called it "Curry Flavored Vegetable Soup."

Everyone loved it and asked me to put it on the menu! Here it is! If no one orders this soup, I swear I will take it off the menu . . .

SO YOU BETTER TRY IT!

Reprinted with permission.

A Food-Friendly Place to Stay

Kingsley Inn
707 Avenue H
Phone: (808) 441-2327; (319) 372-7074

The welcome is warm and the look is classic elegance at the Kingsley Inn in Fort Madison, located across the street from the Mississippi River. Step into the lobby (with its gothic chairs and impressive stairway), and it's hard to believe that the inn was originally a laundry (the fur vault is still in the basement). Constructed in the 1850s, the building was renovated by the Inhance Corporation in 1990 and that same year won the Iowa Governor's Award for The Best Reuse of an Existing Building.

It's no wonder they won such an award. Check out the antique furnishings, stair banisters, railings, and mirrors throughout; zero in on the wallpapers (designer patterns of the type that would have been used during the 1800s). In the spacious bedrooms, you might even want to pay extra attention to the antique headboard. To accommodate queen and/or king size mattresses, several antique headboards—some were originally footboards—had to be heightened.

In the parlor, there's a baby grand piano (it's kept tuned for guests who can play), and in the resplendent Morning Room (where breakfast is served) an elaborate sideboard holds a crystal pitcher of cold lemonade next to a plate of cookies for late afternoon arrivals.

Rates include a full breakfast. Served in the second floor Morning Room, this is no chain hotel's cold cereal and day-old doughnut free-for-all. It's a genteel affair: fruit and yogurt parfaits, excellent quiche, fresh Danish pastries—all cheerfully served to you. Sit in your rosewood chair at one of the antique tables, unfold the thick linen napkin, lift up your heavy silver spoon, and dig in.

It's All in the Name

Both the Kingsley Inn and Alpha's on the Riverfront restaurant were named after Lieutenant Alpha Kingsley, a native of Vermont who was instrumental in the construction of the original Fort Madison in the early 1800s.

skeptical when I heard about the fried strawberries. But in all honesty, if they're in season, the fried strawberries are well worth loosening the belt buckle another notch for. Bite through the fried sugar thin crust to the warm, sweet fruit, add a spoonful of the accompanying real whipped cream, and well, gee, there really is no way to describe the delicate taste sensation other than weirdly, sublimely wonderful.

PS: If you're here and it's not strawberry season, order Kumar's banana fritter with cinnamon ice cream: bananas and rum sauce stuffed within a crispy warm pastry. Yum.

Walt and Jake's Fort Diner
Eighth Street and Avenue H, Phone: (319) 372-1949

The banner says that Walt and Jake's is the home of the Wallyburger, but it could just as well say "Best Breakfast with a View in Fort Madison." From its spotless corner windows, diners can get a panoramic shot of the Mississippi riverfront, Fort Madison's fort, and the trains whistling by.

Still, most folks sit on one of the 11 sittable stools at the counter (the twelfth is a crate set on top of a broken-off pedestal), where listening to the diner banter and watching the cook fry up breakfast or flip pancakes makes a great show too.

This is the quintessential local eat shack, no Disneyland replica—so don't go in expecting fancy schmancy. The servers here are friendly and fun—despite the T-shirt that might state: "I'm a little ORNERY." The place is always busy, and everybody seems to know each other.

Typical of a small-town neighborhood, it's also highly likely during the summer season that there will be garden tomatoes lined up for sale on the counter. In autumn, look for the barrels of red and yellow hot peppers for purchase by the door (the owner grows hundreds of peppers in his home garden). Most importantly, this is also a place where you can expect down-home, damn good food.

Wondering what a Wallyburger really is? Well, it's a pound of ground chuck, piled with sautéed mushrooms and onions, layered with two slices of American cheese and two slices of Swiss cheese. But you can get a "mini" Wallyburger if you want. It's half of everything: a half pound of the ground chuck, a few less mushrooms and onions, and one slice of each of the cheeses. Or how about that Thunder Burger? It's 10 ounces of ground chuck, topped with hot pepper cheese, then smothered in chili and more cheese. Another favorite, the Crazy Cajun, is a mixture of pork sausage and ground chuck, spiked with some hot seasoning over melted hot pepper cheese. These burgers are juicy, tasty, and highly original—no pre-formed patty pulled out of a freezer, fried to a dry finish, and squirted with catsup.

Wallyburgers and Crazy Cajuns aside, I admit morning is still my favorite time to stop in here. That's when you can order Walt's Mess: fresh sausage and green and red peppers grilled with onions and hash browns, topped with American cheese and eggs your style (you can forget the cholesterol counter when you're at Walt and Jake's). Or order the Big Easy: four silver dollar pancakes, two scrambled eggs, biscuit and sausage gravy.

Tuesdays and Saturdays, a local woman delivers pies to the place—and they're the best. One bite of the crust and you know they're made by someone who has been baking pies for a long time. If it's rhubarb season, the perfect pastry is packed with homegrown rhubarb—sweetened just so.

Occasionally, there's a box of cinnamon rolls on the counter; these are from the same baker lady, so don't resist them. Get a couple for down the road, even if you've already stuffed yourself.

The Palms
4920 Avenue O, Phone: (319) 372-5833

The *Des Moines Register* rated The Palms as one of the top 10 places in the state for a steak. But this supper club is worth a visit if for no other reason than it

The Palms in Fort Madison is a classic example of an old-fashioned Midwest supper club.

is such a classic example of a real old-fashioned Midwestern supper club. There's the neon sign out front, there are the palms etched in glass and patterned into the carpet. There's the little waterfall on one side of the room. There are the cocktails. There's the salad bar. There's the seasoned waitress. There's the young couple celebrating their anniversary with shrimp and glasses of wine. There's the family gathered for somebody's birthday.

This is also the first place in Iowa where I experienced the caramel sticky rolls in the bread basket at dinnertime. "I know," the waitress told me, "I was totally amazed the first time I experienced this in a restaurant. But it's not uncommon."

The caramel sticky rolls were incredible, by the way—pull-apart flaky beauties. The salad bar was fresh and appealing. But get here early if you're looking for the prime rib. Sometimes they actually run out.

Be sure to sample some sweet delights at the Ivy Bake Shoppe and Café in Fort Madison.

Ivy Bake Shoppe and Café
622 Seventh Street, Phone: (319) 372-9939

If you want one of the renowned blackberry scones baked and sold here, you need to be at the Ivy on a Thursday and be here early. That's when the blackberry beauties are baked, and when they're gone, they're gone. These lovely delights have been praised by the *Chicago Tribune*, *Time*, and just about everyone in the state of Iowa.

The story of how this successful shop came to be is almost as good as the sweets it sells. In the spring of 1992, the recently divorced Martha Wolf and Susan Welch Saunders (along with three other Fort Madison women) were selling pecan muffins, chocolate mint brownies, apple cake, and other treats on Fridays from Saunders's home to make some extra cash. Customers had to walk through the family room to get to the baked goods, which were displayed on a cloth-covered ping-pong table.

After 18 months, with the bake load increasing crazily, Wolf and Saunders were the only remaining partners. Besides the weekly sale, they had begun supplying treats for three stores.

In 1995, the two moved their booming baking business to this historic three-story red brick building on the corner of Avenue G and Seventh Street in downtown Fort Madison. Nearly 140 years old, the historic structure was once a clothing store—and owned by four generations of the local Hesse family. The old wood floors, big windows, even some display cases and tin ceiling remain, but today folks line up at the counter to purchase pie, not apparel.

Here's how it works: Besides pie, 9x12-inch pans of cakes and bars come out of the ovens in back, get whisked through open cupboard doors to the front, and then are lined up enticingly on the counter like a daily dessert buffet. You're looking at fresh-from-the-oven frosted spice cake, cinnamon-y apple streusel crunch cake, caramel chocolate brownies . . . and more. It's like being at your grandma's annual church potluck picnic back when they still did those sorts of things.

Lunchtime, the Ivy sells soup and tasty sandwiches along with their desserts—and the room is filled with local business people and tourists sitting at big old round dining room tables. Summertime, the screened porch is a nice option.

Faeth Orchards
2469 Highway 2, Phone: (319) 372-1307

Located two miles west of Fort Madison, this is one of my favorite orchards in the state. And I'll freely admit, that could have something to do with Heather Faeth's Stuffed Apple Pie, which I sampled warm from the oven. From its cinnamon sugar-sprinkled flaky pastry to its ultrathin layers of Iowa-grown apples—stacked until no more can fit—the pie is one of the best I've tasted. And, with a five-inch-high middle, it's certainly one of the biggest.

You can buy one of these beauties out at the orchard, where come autumn, the place is bustling. Purchase apples, honey, and cider, preserves and pumpkins, and pick up free recipes throughout the sales rooms for apple bread, cakes, and salad.

The September Seven

During the 1940s and 1950s Herbert Faeth was proud to display the words "Orchard of One Hundred Varieties" in the advertising for his orchard. Through the years, and for many reasons, some of the varieties were not continued. Even so, today, Faeth Orchards grows more than 60 varieties of apples. The following are seven of their September favorites, as described in one of their free recipe handouts at the orchard.

Wealthy. This variety is a tart, crisp eating apple. For those who like apple slices to keep their shape in a pie, the Wealthy is an excellent choice. The apple's appearance is mostly green in color with red "stripes." We mix Wealthy apples with Gala, Beacon, or Honey Gold for a tangy applesauce. Faeth family members do not add sugar to their home cooked applesauce, so we tend to mix varieties for just the right flavor.

Honey Gold. The Honey Gold is one of the Orchard's newest varieties. It is a cross between a Golden Delicious and a Haralson apple developed in Minnesota. It has a somewhat sweet flavor and is a good all-purpose apple. We like Honey Gold slices dipped in caramel.

Gala. For an excellent example of an apple with distinctive yellow coloring and red stripes, check out our Gala apples. This apple hails from New Zealand and when introduced to the United States it became a popular choice. A Gala tastes mildly sweet.

Akane. The Akane variety was introduced in Japan around 1970. It is a cross between a Jonathan and the Worcester Pearmain. It has a tart taste and distinctive aroma. When used in pie the apple slices will keep their shape. When cooked with peel, your applesauce will have a pink color. Its tart taste is appealing in our area. Try slices of the Akane apple with cheddar cheese for dessert or a snack.

Beacon. This is a popular, red summer apple, available in mid-July through mid-September. It is an excellent eating apple and when used in cooking the applesauce has a pink color. We have grown Beacon apples at Faeth Orchards since the late 1940s.

Red Free. This low-acid apple is available in early August. It is medium red in color. Its slightly sweet flavor appeals to our customers. A great apple to pack for lunch or use in your favorite apple bread or cake recipe.

Paula Red. Paula Red apples are bright red on the outside with a white flesh. They are crisp and juicy and good all-purpose apples. They are a McIntosh cross and available earlier than a McIntosh. We use them in apple salad.

Courtesy of Faeth Orchards and reprinted with permission.

Faeth Orchard's Slow Cooker Apple Butter

This recipe is a favorite of the Faeths.

12 to 14 apples (Jerseymac or similar variety)

1 teaspoon cinnamon

2 cups apple cider

2 cups sugar

1/2 teaspoon ground cloves

Chop apples with or without peelings. Place in a slow cooker and add 2 cups cider. Cover and cook 10 to 12 hours on low. Stir once or twice. Run through a strainer if not peeled to remove peels. Add cinnamon and cloves. Cook 4 hours more on high with the lid off until thick. Put into pint or half-pint jars, heat and seal, or cool and freeze.
Courtesy of Faeth Orchards and reprinted with permission.

West Point Sweet Corn Festival

For more than 50 years, on the second weekend of August, the main attraction in West Point is corn, specifically the town's Sweet Corn Festival. An estimated 25,000 show up at this five-day event for the all-you-can eat, hot-buttered sweet stuff—cooked with steam provided by an antique threshing engine. The party starts off with a one-day "Shuck-Fest" followed by four days of barbecue pork chop and chicken dinners, arts and crafts sales, entertainment, tractor pulls, and, of course, contestants squaring off around a table of hot, buttery sweet corn to see who can eat the most.

This is a family-run orchard started in 1853 by Jacob Faeth and his wife Elizabeth Neuschaller, who immigrated to Lee County from Germany. Their son Adam built the original house (circa 1879) that you see as you drive in to the orchard. A master craftsman, he also built the red barn (circa 1883). His wife Anna was said to have sold wagonloads of apples in Fort Madison. The third generation, Herbert (or H.A.), added more buildings to the family farm, including the third barn (now used as the sales room). He truly loved apples (his favorites being the Snow Apple and the Senator), and strove to graft and establish an orchard of a hundred varieties. These days, the fifth generation (the sixth is coming up) is continuing the family's legacy—preserving their historic Iowa family farm and orchard into the twenty-first century.

Franklin

Christian Herschler District Winery and Stagecoach Stop
Sixth and Green Streets, Phone: (319) 835-9432

Set aside a long and languid afternoon for visiting this historic and graceful home located west of Fort Madison and on the edge of a quiet country town.

This is a winery, yes, but it's also a former stagecoach stop that's been restored to its pre-Civil War condition. In fact, it's the only standing registered stagecoach stop in Lee County—part of the Fort Madison to Farmington line.

Lovely gardens surround the place, and after wandering the grounds you can tour the winery, smokehouse room, and the barn. In the house (there's a tour fee for the home), you can view six murals (discovered behind painted walls) from the 1860s that were found when Michael and Lorianne Jarvis began their restoration of the house. All have been restored.

Sit at the heavy wood table in the cool winery, and the Jarvis's will lead you through a taste test of their wines—some made from hundred-year-old

Montrose Watermelon Festival

In 1944, the first Watermelon Festival commenced in the small Mississippi River town of Montrose. At that inaugural affair, Chris Christensen (a successful area melon grower) donated all of the water-melons for the event, and then donated seeds to other farmers who continued to carry on the tradition. Today's festival attendees collectively consume about 10 tons of watermelon over the course of the event, which is held on the last weekend of August.

You can find sweet and juicy Muscatine melons at roadside markets near Muscatine.

Muscatine's Melons

Come August, open-air markets such as Hoope's Melon Shed and Schmidt's Market are filled with the bounty of Muscatine's most well-known crop: melons. No one can explain exactly why the Muscatine melons are among the sweetest and juice-dribbling best. But many attribute it to the fertile farmland in this region that was once an actual island, until the Mississippi River changed its course.

recipes, and many using area fruits. Try the unusual gooseberry (slightly spicy), timeless elderberry blossom, popular rhubarb (great for dessert), plus cherry, Concord (put a quarter cup in your chili for added flavor, says Lorianne), lemon, and more. All are organic, aged in oak barrels for one year.

The vibe is relaxed, and it's fun chatting with a couple so passionate about what they're doing.

Keokuk

Stan's Pastry Shop
814 Main Street, Phone: (319) 524-2991

For a vintage bakery experience, Stan's is the best. This is the type of bakeshop kids return to visit when they're all grown up—bringing along their children.

Open the well-worn screen door, step inside, and you'll understand why. On the counter, plastic bags of fresh angel food cakes are for sale; on shelves in back are bread and buns along with dozens of antique cookie jars. The old-fashioned glass display case is loaded with trays of frosted layer cakes, cream horns, cherry and apple turnovers, date squares, countless cookies, and dozens of doughnuts—including half-moon-shaped ones they call Crescents. One of Stan's bakery specialties, a Crescent is a doughnut cut in half, slathered with buttercream, then topped with the other half of the doughnut.

I'll say the Crescents are delicious, but the real treasure here is their absolutely-not-to-be missed upside-down frosted cupcakes. Why are they frosted upside down? "That's what gives them their own personality," says Lois Waldron, who owns the shop with her husband Stan.

The upside down cupcakes come in a variety of flavors. Try the lemon crunch—with its glazy sugar crust—or the caramel version, or the plain white frosted, or the German chocolate, or my favorite: the Chocolate Marianne, a cocoa cupcake swirled in chocolate frosting then finished off with a dollop of white buttercream. The whole thing is sweetly and messily over the top—even if it's upside down.

Stan's Pastry Shop in Keokuk offers a vintage bakery experience.

That's not all. Stan's is also famous for its cream horns. Take a look at the wall where photos of friends holding and/or eating Stan's cream horns appear from around the world. Pictures have been sent from California, Washington, D.C., the Hoover Dam, New York, and Iceland. The photos all started when a Keokuk student wanted his parents to bring him Stan's cream horns while he was in Egypt.

Stan's has been a family affair (all seven of the Waldron children helped work in the bakery at one time or another) since the Waldrons bought the Keokuk shop in 1967, but Stan was in the bakery business long before that. He bought his first sweet shop in Anamosa, Iowa, when he was just 19 years old.

Liz Clark's
116 Concert Street, Phone: (319) 524-4716

You have to plan ahead if you want to dine at Liz's. But trust me, it's worth it. This is one of those dining experiences you don't get to partake in very often. For one thing, her restaurant, an elegant and beautifully renovated Italianate house (built in the mid-1800s) is also her home.

The setting is only a part of the feast, though. Dinner here means a several-course meal (served for two or up to 36 seated) prepared by Liz. An accomplished chef, she's studied cooking in Italy and France and has been named by various publications as one of the Midwest's best chefs.

A typical dinner menu might feature delicacies such as tuna tartar for starters, roasted red pepper soup, a main course of roasted quail with truffle sauce, braised endive, and oven-roasted fingerling potatoes. Dessert? How about perfect poached pears on fresh pear sorbet with caramel sauce?

Besides her reservation-only dinner parties, Liz Clark also operates a cooking school with classes for both beginning and advanced students that feature recipes ranging from Spanish tapas to American barbecue to French berry desserts. Over the years, her many creations have also included recipes using some of Iowa's most famous foods, including her two favorite cuts of pork, the loin chop and the tenderloin (see the sidebar for one of her great recipes).

Liz Clark's Pork Favorites

Chef and cooking instructor LizClark says her favorite way to fix pork is really quite simple. "Pour flour on a plate, season it with sea salt, cayenne, and cinnamon." (You can use this mixture for fried chicken too.) Dip a thin-cut, bone-in loin chop in the mixture. Then fry it up in bacon fat. "When it's done, you can chew it right down to the bone. It's even good for breakfast," she says.

Her other favorite cut of pork is the tenderloin. "It's really the most elegant cut of pork, sauces beautifully, and goes with anything." Here's an example.

Pork Tenderloins, with Coffee Cream Sauce

2 whole true pork tenders*

3 tablespoons butter

1 cup strong black coffee

1/4 cup brandy

1 cup whipping cream

Sea salt, freshly grated nutmeg, and freshly ground pepper to taste
The pork tender is the small portion that runs along the loin. In the grocery store, they're usually about 12 inches long with a diameter of 2 to 3 inches—and are labeled as tenderloin.

Preheat oven to 400 degrees.

Tie the small end of the tenderloins under the loin to give uniform size to the loin.

In a heavy enameled skillet, over medium high heat, melt the butter. Brown the tenderloins on all sides. Remove them to a rack in a roasting pan and place in the preheated oven to continue cooking for 15 to 20 minutes, or until juices run pink and internal temperature is 140 degrees. Remove to a cutting board and allow to rest for 15 minutes.

Add the coffee and brandy to the skillet and bring to a boil, scraping the bottom with a wooden spatula to remove all browned bits. Reduce until only 3 to 4 tablespoons of liquid remain. Add the whipping cream and bring to a boil. Reduce by half. Sauce should thicken and coat the spatula. Season to taste with salt, nutmeg, and pepper.

Slice the tenderloin on the diagonal into half-inch-thick slices. Arrange on plates and serve with some of the sauce poured over.

Serves 4 to 6.

Fresh Corn Salsa

4 ears fresh sweet corn, cleaned

4 medium ripe tomatoes, peeled, seeded, and chopped

2 small jalapeño pepper, ribs and seeds removed, chopped

2 tablespoons minced fresh cilantro

1 small red onion, peeled and diced

Olive oil to moisten

3 to 4 tablespoons sherry wine vinegar

Sea salt and freshly ground black pepper to taste

Taste corn for sweetness. (If corn is starting to taste starchy, roast until slightly charred in grill pan heated to high.) Cut corn kernels from cobs.

In a medium bowl, mix corn kernels, tomatoes, jalapeño pepper, cilantro, red onion. Moisten with olive oil and sherry wine vinegar. Season to taste with sea salt and freshly ground black pepper.

Serves 16.

Courtesy of Liz Clark and reprinted with permission.

Smiles and homegrown sweet corn naturally go together in Iowa.

Liz Clark's 10 Iowa Food Favorites

Liz Clark is a renowned chef, and the author of several cookbooks including *Fresh Bread Companion*, *Apple Companion*, and *Cranberry Companion*.

Sage Restaurant, Des Moines

Embassy Club, Des Moines. Non-members can call for reservations; also **Saturday morning Farmers' Market, Keokuk**

Amana Meat Shop and Smokehouse, Amana. For cured meats

Stringtown Market, Kalona. For bulk grocery items

Aoeshe Japanese Restaurant, Iowa City

Cellar Restaurant, Keokuk. For a noontime hamburger

New Pioneer Co-op, Iowa City. For organic meat and produce

Dave's Old Fashioned Meats, Montrose. For great meats

Hy-Vee Grocery Store, Keokuk. An extremely well-stocked market

Index by City

Index by Type of Establishment

MORE GREAT TITLES
FROM TRAILS BOOKS
& PRAIRIE OAK PRESS

ACTIVITY GUIDES

Biking Wisconsin: 50 Great Road and Trail Rides, *Steve Johnson*

Great Cross-Country Ski Trails: Wisconsin, Minnesota, Michigan & Ontario,
Wm. Chad McGrath

Great Iowa Walks: 50 Strolls, Rambles, Hikes, and Treks, *Lynn L. Walters*

Great Minnesota Walks: 49 Strolls, Rambles, Hikes, and Treks, *Wm. Chad McGrath*

Great Wisconsin Walks: 45 Strolls, Rambles, Hikes, and Treks, *Wm. Chad McGrath*

Horsing Around in Wisconsin, *Anne M. Connor*

Iowa Underground, *Greg A. Brick*

Minnesota Underground & the Best of the Black Hills, *Doris Green*

Paddling Illinois: 64 Great Trips by Canoe and Kayak, *Mike Svob*

Paddling Iowa: 96 Great Trips by Canoe and Kayak, *Nate Hoogeveen*

Paddling Northern Minnesota: 86 Great Trips by Canoe and Kayak,
Lynne Smith Diebel

Paddling Northern Wisconsin: 82 Great Trips by Canoe and Kayak, *Mike Svob*

Paddling Southern Wisconsin: 82 Great Trips by Canoe and Kayak, *Mike Svob*

Walking Tours of Wisconsin's Historic Towns, *Lucy Rhodes,
Elizabeth McBride, Anita Matcha*

Wisconsin's Outdoor Treasures: A Guide to 150 Natural Destinations, *Tim Bewer*

Wisconsin Underground, *Doris Green*

TRAVEL GUIDES

Classic Wisconsin Weekends, *Michael Bie*

Great Little Museums of the Midwest, *Christine des Garennes*

Great Midwest Country Escapes, *Nina Gadomski*

Great Minnesota Taverns, *David K. Wright & Monica G. Wright*

Great Minnesota Weekend Adventures, *Beth Gauper*

Great Weekend Adventures, *the Editors of Wisconsin Trails*

Great Wisconsin Romantic Weekends, *Christine des Garennes*

Great Wisconsin Taverns: 101 Distinctive Badger Bars, *Dennis Boyer*

Iowa's Hometown Flavors, *Donna Tabbert Long*

Sacred Sites of Minnesota, *John-Brian Paprock & Teresa Peneguy Paprock*

Sacred Sites of Wisconsin, *John-Brian Paprock & Teresa Peneguy Paprock*

Tastes of Minnesota: A Food Lover's Tour, *Donna Tabbert Long*

The Great Iowa Touring Book: 27 Spectacular Auto Trips, *Mike Whye*

The Great Minnesota Touring Book: 30 Spectacular Auto Trips, *Thomas Huhti*

The Great Wisconsin Touring Book: 30 Spectacular Auto Tours, *Gary Knowles*

Wisconsin Family Weekends: 20 Fun Trips for You and the Kids,
Susan Lampert Smith

Wisconsin Golf Getaways, *Jeff Mayers and Jerry Poling*

Wisconsin Lighthouses: A Photographic and Historical Guide,
Ken and Barb Wardius
Wisconsin's Hometown Flavors, *Terese Allen*
Wisconsin Waterfalls, *Patrick Lisi*
Up North Wisconsin: A Region for All Seasons, *Sharyn Alden*

HOME & GARDEN

Bountiful Wisconsin: 110 Favorite Recipes, *Terese Allen*
Codfather 2, *Jeff Hagen*
Creating a Perennial Garden in the Midwest, *Joan Severa*
Eating Well in Wisconsin, *Jerry Minnich*
Foods That Made Wisconsin Famous: 150 Great Recipes, *Richard J. Baumann*
Midwest Cottage Gardening, *Frances Manos*
North Woods Cottage Cookbook, *Jerry Minnich*
Wisconsin Country Gourmet, *Marge Snyder & Suzanne Breckenridge*
Wisconsin Garden Guide, *Jerry Minnich*

HISTORICAL BOOKS

Barns of Wisconsin, *Jerry Apps*
Duck Hunting on the Fox: Hunting and Decoy-Carving Traditions,
Stephen M. Miller
Grand Army of the Republic: Department of Wisconsin, *Thomas J. McCrory*
Portrait of the Past: A Photographic Journey Through Wisconsin 1865-1920,
Howard Mead, Jill Dean, and Susan Smith
Prairie Whistles: Tales of Midwest Railroading, *Dennis Boyer*
Shipwrecks of Lake Michigan, *Benjamin J. Shelak*
Wisconsin At War: 20th Century Conflicts Through the Eyes of Veterans, *Dr. James
F. McIntosh, M.D.*
Wisconsin's Historic Houses & Living History Museums, *Krista Finstad Hanson*
Wisconsin: The Story of the Badger State, *Norman K. Risjord*

GIFT BOOKS

Celebrating Door County's Wild Places, *The Ridges Sanctuary*
Fairlawn: Restoring the Splendor, *Tom Davis*
Madison, *Photography by Brent Nicastro*
Milwaukee, *Photography by Todd Dacquisto*
Milwaukee Architecture: A Guide to Notable Buildings, *Joseph Korom*
Spirit of the North: A Photographic Journey Through Northern Wisconsin, *Richard
Hamilton Smith*
The Spirit of Door County: A Photographic Essay, *Darryl R. Beers*
Uncommon Sense: The Life Of Marshall Erdman, *Doug Moe & Alice D'Alessio*

LEGENDS & LORE

Driftless Spirits: Ghosts of Southwest Wisconsin, *Dennis Boyer*
Haunted Wisconsin, *Michael Norman and Beth Scott*

The Beast of Bray Road: Tailing Wisconsin's Werewolf, *Linda S. Godfrey*
The Eagle's Voice: Tales Told by Indian Effigy Mounds, *Gary J. Maier, M.D.*
The Poison Widow: A True Story of Sin, Strychnine, & Murder, *Linda S. Godfrey*
The W-Files: True Reports of Wisconsin's Unexplained Phenomena, *Jay Rath*

YOUNG READERS

ABCs Naturally, *Lynne Smith Diebel & Jann Faust Kalscheur*
ABCs of Wisconsin, *Dori Hillestad Butler, Illustrated by Alison Relyea*
H is for Hawkeye, *Jay Wagner, Illustrated by Eileen Potts Dawson*
H is for Hoosier, *Dori Hillestad Butler, Illustrated by Eileen Potts Dawson*
Wisconsin Portraits, *Martin Hintz*
Wisconsin Sports Heroes, *Martin Hintz*
W is for Wisconsin, *Dori Hillestad Butler, Illustrated by Eileen Potts Dawson*

SPORTS

Baseball in Beertown: America's Pastime in Milwaukee, *Todd Mishler*
Before They Were the Packers: Green Bay's Town Team Days,
Denis J. Gullickson & Carl Hanson
Cold Wars: 40+ Years of Packer-Viking Rivalry, *Todd Mishler*
Downfield: Untold Stories of the Green Bay Packers, *Jerry Poling*
Great Moments in Wisconsin Sports, *Todd Mishler*
Green Bay Packers Titletown Trivia Teasers, *Don Davenport*
Mean on Sunday: The Autobiography of Ray Nitschke, *Robert W. Wells*
Mudbaths and Bloodbaths: The Inside Story of the Bears-Packers Rivalry,
Gary D'Amato & Cliff Christl
Packers By the Numbers: Jersey Numbers and the Players Who Wore Them,
John Maxymuk

OTHER

Driftless Stories, *John Motoviloff*
River Stories: Growing Up on the Wisconsin, *Delores Chamberlain*
The Wisconsin Father's Guide to Divorce, *James Novak*
Travels With Sophie: The Journal of Louise E. Wegner,
Edited by Gene L. LaBerge & Michelle L. Maurer
Trout Friends, *Bill Stokes*
Wild Wisconsin Notebook, *James Buchholz*

For a free catalog, phone, write, or e-mail us.

Trails Books

P.O. Box 317, Black Earth, WI 53515
(800) 236-8088 • e-mail: books@wistrails.com